THE
HUNK
COOKBOOK

Mary Anne Bauer

A Nitty Gritty® Cookbook

Printed in the United States of America.

ISBN 0-911954-93-7

Production Consultant:
    Vicki L. Crampton
Photo Stylist: Ken Hoyt
Photographer: Kathryn Opp
Food Stylist:
    Carol Cooper Ladd
Assistant to Food Stylist:
    Barbara Brooks
Illustrator: Carol Webb Atherly

Special thanks to Terry Krebser for the
1958 Chevy Impala convertible used in
the photograph on page 67 and to the
Horsebrass Pub for the props used in
the photograph on page 31.

Table of Contents

Acknowledgements

A special thank you to the people who sent us recipes and inspiration for recipes.

Harold Aichholz
American Lamb Council
Roger Aust
Edwin Baldree
Frank Barnett
Martin Blohn
Charles Boynton
Patty Brandt
Terry Brandt
Duane Brown
Ed Bystran
Peter R. Chamberlain
Sam Christie
Tom Codekas
Dale Collins
Juan Daviess
Dan Davis
Patrick Dunlevy
Michael Durrell
Curt Edwards
Steve Eldredge
Paul Farrow
George Fisher
Milford Ford
Rick Freeland
Dr. John Furlong
Charles Gardiner
Phillip Gibbona
Art Gleason
Nelson Graham

William H. Green
John Gregos
Phil Grove
Anthony Guardino
Roy Hanson
Helen Hardeman
David Harper
Steve Harris
Jim Hessel
Ron Holmgren
Jordan Humble
Gevona Jones
Joe Kaleel
Joe Kill
Brook Kirklin
Dennis Kringer
Ellie Kringer
Adrienne Lee
Mrs. Lee
Kenneth J. Levstone
Ray Lund
John Marcoules
Chef Horst Mager
David T. McDonald
Malcolm McDonald
Les McNary
Lou Meyer
Gertrude Murphy
Lynn S. Murry
Warren Niete

Ken Ooley
Oregon Beef Council
Oregon Chapter of American
   Heart Association
Oregon Dairy Commission
Oregon Dairy Council
John Peck
Rudolph Prael
Michael Reed
J. Michael Reid
The Rheinlander Restaurant
Mrs. Riley
Larry Roberts
Robert W. Rothman
Cheryl Russel
Jesse Sanders
The Sea Hag Restaurant
   (Chef Brett Meisner)
Marilyn Senko
James D. Smith
Marybeth Stiner
Surf Restaurant
Ed Swanda
Nick Talbot
Dennis Taylor
Greg Toran
Jim Towns
Steve Tuttle
Robert Vattiat
Woodstock Wine and Deli

Special Thanks to: Pat O'Holleran, Lorraine Johnston and Marilyn Senko who assisted with distribution of surveys throughout the country.

Introduction

To develop a cookbook full of foods men love, we went directly to the source. We launched the project with a Northwest Men's Recipe Contest, giving us not only a great start on this book, but an impressive and sometimes surprising awareness of men's interest, understanding and real passion for food.

Our next task was to develop a survey, which we distributed to 4000 men throughout the United States. These men provided a wealth of information on what's hot and what's not. Information-gathering did not stop with the survey, however. Once the word was out that such a project was underway, everybody had an opinion to add.

Some of the information was predictable. The food that appeared first on more than 75% of the "Foods Men Avoid" list was liver. (Less predictable was the most disliked vegetable, Brussels sprouts.) Also as expected, many men are confirmed meat and potato devotees. And we're not surprised at the news that the barbecue is man's best friend when he is called on to do the food preparation. But some of the responses showed a new male profile emerging.

Many men like to cook in the kitchen as well as on the barbecue. They are interested in cooking almost every kind of food, although breakfast and stir-frying were mentioned most often. A wealth of recipes in this book come from men, and will give you an idea of how capable they are becoming in the culinary department.

Although many men still go for rich foods, more and more men are becoming health-conscious. When we included a place on our survey for men to list foods they avoid, we gave them a chance to tell us whether they avoided them for health reasons or for taste preference. More than expected, men listed items they avoided because they were less healthy than other foods.

Salads and vegetables were high on the list of men's favored foods, perhaps as a consequence of their new awareness of what is good for them. And caffeine seems to be on the wane, at least in coffee , which was almost never mentioned as the favorite beverage.

We'll give you more information on our surveys as you browse through our "Hunk Cookbook," enjoying the beautiful men who consented to decorate our kitchens while we cook, and trying all of the recipes, both traditional and new, for foods that men love.

Appetizers and Snacks

From midday munchies to midnight noshes, appetizers and snacks are important male food fare. Men love to snack, whether it's nibbling while watching TV or playing cards, or "a little something before dinner."

And when the snack attacks occur, men enjoy everyday snacks such as popcorn, peanuts, cheese and crackers and nachos, or for more epicurian moments, even escargot and chicken liver paté.

Appetizers scoring the highest included shrimp as the number one champ, chicken wings as an enthusiastic second place winner, and Mexican style foods such as nachos in third place. So we've gathered the best of shrimp with **Marinated Shrimp**, and tempted the chicken wing lovers with an outstanding array of wonderful wing snacks. We've added **Not So Macho Nachos**, **Year 'Round Salsa** and **Mexicali Bean Dip** so he'll be ready for the most commanding snack attack.

The men who cook approach the area of appetizers with gusto, from **Ron's Wontons** to **Seafood Salad Spread.** They're working for rave reviews from their guests, and getting them!

Popcorn

Popcorn is the favorite snack mentioned most often by men all over the country. Plain old popcorn is great, but why not dress up the white stuff with some variations?

Variations: Stir any of the following into melted butter (all to taste, of course) before pouring over popcorn and tossing to coat.

- **Seasoned Popcorn.** Add seasoning salt.
- **Italian Popcorn.** Add Good Seasons dressing mix.
- **Ranch Popcorn.** Add ranch dressing mix.
- **Chili Popcorn.** Add chili powder.
- **Cheddar Popcorn.** Add shredded sharp cheddar cheese.
- **Lemon Pepper Popcorn.** Add lemon pepper spice.
- **Pumpkin Popcorn.** Add pumpkin pie spice.
- **Bacon Popcorn.** Add cooked, crumbled bacon after tossing popcorn in melted butter.
- **Hot and Spicy Popcorn.** Add drops of Tabasco sauce.
- **Garlic Popcorn.** Add garlic powder.
- **Maple Syrup Cinnamon Popcorn.** Add maple syrup and cinnamon.
- **Fruit and Nut Popcorn.** Add apple pie spices, toss popcorn in flavored butter, and then add dried apple, toasted slivered almonds, raisins or mixed dried fruit bits.
- **Curried Popcorn.** Add mild curry powder to butter and toss. Then add golden raisins, flaked coconut and salted peanuts.
- **Chocolate Popcorn.** Add chocolate chips or other sweet chips (peanut butter chips, butterscotch chips, mint chocolate chips) after tossing popcorn in butter.

Barbecued Nuts

3 cups

This is an easy way to make yourself popular with the important snacker in your life. Easy for a party, too.

3 cups unsalted peanuts **or** almonds
¼ cup barbecue sauce

In a small bowl, stir together nuts and sauce until nuts are evenly coated. Spread on a lightly greased baking sheet. Bake 10-15 minutes at 300°. Cool and store in an airtight container. Keeps indefinitely.

Chicken Liver Paté

2 cups

Terry prepares this recipe and serves it proudly to guests. It has become his specialty. The unique combination of apples and dates gives the perfect touch of sweetness.

1 lb. chicken livers
1½ cups port wine
2 medium red delicious apples, peeled, chopped
1 onion, chopped
6 dates, pitted
½ tsp. salt
⅛ tsp. cayenne pepper

In a medium saucepan, cook chicken livers in ⅔ cup of port wine 10 minutes or just until pink. Do not overcook. Cut chicken livers into small pieces and set aside. Sauté apples, onions and dates in ⅓ cup wine for about 10 minutes. Add salt and pepper. Add chicken livers and remaining ½ cup wine. Cover and cook over medium heat 3 minutes, stirring occasionally. Remove from heat and cool 10 minutes. Place contents in a blender or food processor and puree until very smooth. Pour into a serving bowl or crock, cover with plastic wrap and refrigerate at least 6 hours. Will keep, refrigerated, for 2 days.

Ron's Wontons

Ron has mastered his now famous wonton recipe, and is asked to prepare them for every gathering. He uses his food processor to quickly chop the cabbage, water chestnuts and garlic. Ron says he usually doubles or triples the recipe so he can freeze some for later.

½ lb. lean ground beef
1 stalk Chinese cabbage (4 large leaves, white stems removed)
3 water chestnuts
1 clove garlic

¼ tsp. fresh ginger, chopped
1 tsp. sesame oil
1½ tbs. soy sauce
1 pkg. wonton wrappers

In a food processor, chop cabbage leaves, water chestnuts and garlic. In a medium bowl, mix ground beef, chopped cabbage mixture, ginger, sesame oil and soy sauce. Knead together. Place 1 tbs. filling in the center of a wonton wrapper. Moisten edges with water. Fold diagonally, then fold points to center — like a diaper! Heat oil to 375°. Deep fry until golden brown. Serve with a favorite sauce, catsup or mustard. Reheat frozen wontons in a 400° oven for 5 minutes.

Tip: Wonton wrappers are available in the produce section of most grocery stores.

Quick Barbecued Chicken Wings

Chicken wings were named as a favorite appetizer among men throughout the country. Here's the first of three variations on the theme.

2 lbs. chicken wings, disjointed with tips removed
1 cup bottled, hickory-smoked barbecue sauce

Spray a 9" x 13" baking pan with vegetable coating. Arrange wings in a single layer and cover each with barbecue sauce. Bake at 350° for 45 minutes. Serve hot.

Year 'Round Salsa

Ingredients for this great tasting salsa are always available, so Martin enjoys preparing this delightful recipe anytime.

2 cups frozen whole kernel corn
2 cups fresh tomatoes, peeled, seeded, diced
¾ cup onion, diced
¾ cup green bell pepper, diced
½ cup fresh cilantro, chopped

⅓ cup lime juice
1½ tsp. ground cumin
1 tbs. chili powder
2 cloves garlic, finely minced
1 tsp. salt

Prepare frozen corn according to package directions, cooking only 2 minutes or until crunchy tender. Drain. Place corn and tomatoes in a medium bowl. Drain any accumulated liquid from tomato and corn mixture. Stir in onion, pepper and cilantro. In a separate bowl, mix lime juice, cumin, chili powder, garlic and salt together. Add to tomato-corn mixture. Cover and chill. May be served immediately or refrigerated for several days. Serve with corn chips.

Variation: Use this salsa as a condiment on tacos or with broiled meat and poultry.

Sweet and Sour Chicken Wings

A touch of Chinese flavors this variation.

2-3 lbs chicken wings
2 cups catsup
2 tbs. Worcestershire sauce
2 tbs. brown sugar

2 tbs. vinegar
2 tsp. soy sauce
1 cup crushed pineapple, drained

In a small bowl, mix all ingredients except chicken wings. Place wings in a 9" x 13" baking pan and pour sauce over all. Bake at 350° for 45 minutes. Serve hot.

Parmesan Chicken Wings

20-30 wings

Add a little Italian flavor with this crispy variety.

2-3 lbs. chicken wings
¼ lb. (1 stick) butter or margarine, melted
1 cup Parmesan cheese, grated

1 tsp. garlic powder
1 tsp. Italian seasoning

In a shallow bowl, mix Parmesan cheese, garlic powder and seasoning. Dip chicken wings into melted butter and then into cheese and seasoning mixture. Place on a greased cookie sheet and bake at 350° for 45 minutes.

Instant Cream Cheese Spreads

1½-2½ cups

Turn a humble block of cream cheese into an elegant hors d'oeuvre instantly. Or try cream cheese spread ideas. Serve with an assortment of crackers. English water biscuits are especially nice.

Place an 8 oz. pkg. of cream cheese on a glass plate. Then top with any of the following:

- ½ cup seafood sauce and 1 cup small shrimp, sprinkled with fresh parsley
- ½ cup seafood sauce and 1 cup crab meat
- ½ cup chutney, sprinkled with slivered almonds
- 1 cup jalapeno jelly
- 1 cup mint jelly
- 1 cup whole cranberry relish

Or try these cream cheese spread ideas. Mix the following with 3 ozs. of cream cheese at room temperature.

- 1 (3 ozs.) can of ham spread, 2 tbs. sour cream, 3 tbs. chopped water chestnuts and 1 tsp. horseradish.
- 3 ozs. Roquefort cheese, 1 tbs. white wine, 2 tbs. minced onion and ½ cup pistachio nuts, chopped.

Ham Wheels

25 pieces

Make these eye-appealing nibbles ahead of time. Canned green chili strips can be substituted for a taste and color variation.

1 (4 ozs.) pkg. Danish ham (5 slices)
4 ozs. light cream cheese
1 (7 ozs.) jar roasted red peppers

Pat each slice of ham dry on paper towels. Thinly spread with cream cheese. Pat peppers dry on paper towels and cut into ⅜" wide strips. Place a strip of pepper along a narrow side of the ham slice, and then 4-5 more strips parallel to the first one, spaced at ¾" intervals. Leave a ¾" border at the top. Roll into a tight roll and refrigerate for at least an hour to firm. Just before serving, cut each roll into 5 pieces, and arrange "pretty side" up.

Artichoke Non-Quiche

16 squares

Real men eat non-quiche. (They also eat quiche!) This recipe is from Larry.

2 (6 ozs. each) marinated artichokes, chopped, oil reserved
1 small onion, chopped
1 garlic clove, minced
4 eggs
6 soda crackers, crumbled
½ lb. cheddar cheese, grated
dash Tabasco
¼ cup parsley, chopped
salt and freshly ground pepper

Sauté onion and garlic in artichoke oil. In a medium bowl, beat eggs, add remaining ingredients and mix. Pour into an 8" x 8" square pan. Bake at 375° for 30 minutes. After cooling, cut into squares. Serve at room temperature.

Mexicali Bean Dip

No matter how much of this one you make, there will never be enough!

1 lb. lean ground beef
1 large onion, chopped
½ (10 ozs.) bottle hot catsup
3 tsp. chili powder, or to taste
1 tsp. salt
2 (8 ozs. each) cans kidney beans, 1 drained, 1 with liquid, pureed in a
  food processor or blender
1 cup sharp cheddar cheese, shredded
½ cup black olives, chopped
tortilla chips

In a hot skillet, fry ground beef and ½ cup of the chopped onion. Add pureed beans, hot catsup, chili powder and salt. Turn heat to low and simmer, uncovered, 15-20 minutes. Distribute cheese, remaining onion and chopped olive evenly over meat-bean mixture. Cover and simmer until cheese melts. Serve hot in skillet with tortilla chips.

Classic Shrimp Cocktail Sauce

for 1 lb. shrimp

From every corner of the country, shrimp cocktail was appetizer #1. This classic sauce will work with crab and oysters as well.

1 cup catsup
3 tbs. fresh lemon juice
⅓ cup celery, finely chopped
½ tsp. Worcestershire sauce
2 tsp. prepared white horseradish
⅛ tsp. finely ground white pepper

Combine ingredients in a small bowl and chill in the refrigerator for 1-2 hours until ready to serve shrimp.

The Sea Hag's Marinated Shrimp

Serves 6-8

Everyone loves an evening at The Sea Hag restaurant at Lincoln City, where the owner plays the bottles at the bar several times a night to the delight of guests. The marinated shrimp is an appetizer savored by fishermen as well as diners who flock in from all parts of the country to enjoy this specialty of the house.

3 lbs. fresh shrimp in the shell
⅓ cup salt
1 onion, sliced
½ cup vinegar

½ cup water
¾ cup brown sugar
⅓ cup white wine
1 tbs. pickling spices

In a large pan, cover shrimp with water, add salt and bring to a boil. Cook 2-3 minutes, or just until shrimp turn pink. Drain and rinse in cold water immediately. When cooled, place in a glass container with a cover, layering shrimp and sliced onion. In a medium saucepan, mix vinegar, water, brown sugar, wine and pickling spices. Bring just to a boil; cool slightly and pour over shrimp while hot. Refrigerate overnight. Remove shrimp from marinade and serve on a plate or plates lined with lettuce leaves.

Easy Marinated Shrimp

Serves 6-8

*Shrimp is **the** most popular appetizer among men. This one is simple and delicious.*

1 cup bottled Italian salad dressing
1 lb. shrimp, cooked, shelled

In a saucepan or microwave dish, heat salad dressing until hot but not boiling. Place shrimp in a shallow bowl and pour hot dressing over all. Allow to marinate in the refrigerator several hours. Serve with toothpicks.

Tip: Marinated shrimp are also a flavorful addition to an elegant tossed salad.

Seafood Salad Spread

Edwin tells us that rave reviews always accompany this delicious yet easy to prepare hors d'oeuvre.

2 cups (1 lb.) crab meat
1 cup cooked shrimp, cut into small pieces
3 cups celery, diced
2 hard-boiled eggs, finely chopped
1 cup mayonnaise
1 small onion, finely chopped
salt and freshly ground pepper

In a medium bowl, combine crab meat, shrimp, celery and eggs. Mix mayonnaise, onion, salt and pepper. Pour over mixture and gently toss. Cover and chill at least 2 hours. Thin with a bit more mayonnaise if necessary. Delicious on crackers.

Variations:
- Add sliced water chestnuts.
- Add slivered almonds.

Tip: This recipe is also delicious as a light first course, served in a scooped-out tomato or on a lettuce leaf. Or for a light entrée, place in a casserole, top with buttered bread crumbs and bake at 350° for 15-20 minutes until heated through.

Stuffed Mushrooms

Stuffed mushrooms are the second highest rated appetizer among men surveyed, so be sure to prepare plenty of these creamy gems.

25-30 medium mushrooms
¾ lb. bacon
2 tbs. onion, minced
1 (8 ozs.) pkg. cream cheese

½ cup Parmesan cheese, grated
1 tbs. milk or cream
¼ cup butter, melted
2-3 tbs. parsley, minced

Remove mushroom stems. Chop finely and set aside. Fry bacon, drain well and crumble. Remove all but 1 tbs. fat from pan. Add onion and chopped mushroom stems. Sauté until soft; remove and drain on paper towels. In a small bowl, mix cream cheese, Parmesan cheese and milk or cream. Add crumbled bacon and sautéed onion and mushroom stems. Mix well. Dip mushrooms into melted butter to coat and place on a cookie sheet. Stuff with filling, mounding in center. Bake in a 350° oven 10 to 12 minutes. Sprinkle with parsley and serve.

Joe's Marinated Mushrooms

Serves 4-6

Joe keeps a jar of these on hand to add to salads or serve for munchies when friends stop by for a quick beer.

1 lb. small button mushrooms
½ cup olive oil
3 cloves garlic, smashed
½ cup rice wine vinegar **or** cider vinegar
¼ tsp. red pepper flakes

2 tbs. lemon juice
½ tsp. sugar
1 tsp. dried thyme
1 tsp. dried sweet basil
salt and freshly ground pepper

In a medium saucepan, combine all ingredients except mushrooms. Bring to a boil and simmer over low heat for 5 minutes. Trim stems off mushrooms. If mushrooms are large, cut them into quarters; if small, just trim caps. Place in saucepan with olive oil and vinegar mixture. Simmer for 5 minutes, stirring occasionally. Remove from heat and let mushrooms cool in liquid. Place mushrooms in a glass jar, pour marinade over and cover tightly. Refrigerate until ready to use. These keep well for about a week.

Pesto Puffs

Male guests always love this puffy, golden, hot hors d'oeuvre. Pesto makes this extra special and the ham or turkey and cheese variation is a great way to serve a favorite combination.

1 pkg. puff pastry sheets
2 tbs. pesto
thinly sliced ham
Monterey Jack or provolone cheese
2 eggs
2 tbs. water

Remove frozen puff pastry sheets 20 or 30 minutes before preparing puffs. On a lightly floured board, roll pastry sheet until it measures 18" x 12". Cut down the middle. Place the first half on a cookie sheet. Spread pesto thinly over entire sheet, leaving ½" around edge for joining. Place a layer of cheese over pesto followed by a layer of ham. Place second layer of puff on top. Join top and bottom pieces of pastry together using water to moisten. Fold ½" of edges over and use a fork to seal them together. Repeat with second sheet of pastry. Using a sharp knife, cut a design of tiny cuts all over top pastry. At this point, puffs may be covered with plastic wrap and refrigerated up to 2 days before baking. Or, double wrap and freeze up to 4 weeks. To bake: brush puff with egg wash made by beating 2 eggs with 2 tbs. water. Allow to dry and brush again. Bake in a 425° oven, about 15 minutes or until puffed and golden. Cut into squares and serve warm.

Not So Macho Nachos

Serves 2-4

A microwave oven makes this an instant treat when he's got a taste for something Mexican.

24 large tortilla chips
1 cup cheddar cheese, shredded **or** Monterey Jack
⅓ cup black olives, sliced
1 tbs. canned jalapeno peppers, sliced or chopped

Gently toss tortilla chips with cheese, olives and peppers. Pour onto a microwave-safe plate. Microwave on medium (50% power) for 2-4 minutes or until cheese is melted, turning plate once or twice. Serve immediately.

Variation: Spread ½-1 tsp. refried beans on each tortilla chip before sprinkling with cheese. Top with 3 tbs. chopped onion, olives and pepper. Cook as directed and top with chopped fresh tomato or salsa before serving.

Tip: If you always toss your chips with ingredients before you warm them, there will be cheese on the chips at the bottom of the pile as well as the top!

Beverages

The news surprised us a little. In our surveys men favored tea first, nearly tied with beer. Milk was a close third, and water and cola followed. Very little mention was made of coffee, our first surprise. A lot of men just said "Water," another unpredicted response. And many sent recipes, some of the best included here.

Poolside Party Punch

Gather friends around the pool — or anywhere! — for a cool summer punch.

1 (6 oz.) can orange juice concentrate
1 (6 oz.) can frozen lemonade concentrate
3 cups cold water
1 (750 ml) bottle champagne, chilled
sliced strawberries **or** peaches, oranges, or pineapple

In a large pitcher, mix orange juice concentrate, lemonade concentrate and water. Chill. To serve: pour over a block of ice in a punchbowl, add chilled champagne, and float fruit slices.

Variation: Add ginger ale in place of champagne.

Frozen Strawberry Daiquiris

Milford is always the popular host with his delicious party drink.

1⅓ cups crushed ice
¾ cup light rum
¼ cup fresh lime juice
¼ cup Creme de Cassis liqueur
½ tsp. sugar
24 medium strawberries, sliced
4 large strawberries with stems for garnish

Place ice, rum, lime juice, Creme de Cassis, sugar and sliced strawberries in blender. Blend 10 seconds or until slushy. Pour into 4 stemmed glasses. Make a slit in whole berries and hang on rims of glasses.

Margaritas

*If the food is Mexican, and even if it isn't, this is the **best** margarita for the occasion.*

1 lime or lemon
coarse salt
1 cup Tequila
1 (6 ozs.) can frozen limeade concentrate

½ cup Triple Sec
juice of 1 lemon
1 egg white
2 cups crushed ice

Cut lime or lemon in half and rub glass rim. Dip rims in finely ground salt. In a blender, combine remaining ingredients. Serve in stemmed margarita glasses.

Favorite Eggnog

Terry loves to entertain, and this rich eggnog is a favorite, especially during the holidays.

12 egg yolks
1 cup sugar
2 cups bourbon whiskey
1 cup brandy
12 egg whites

1 tsp. salt
1 qt. milk
1 pt. cream, whipped
ground nutmeg

In a large bowl, beat egg yolks with sugar until thick and lemon-colored. Slowly add bourbon and brandy. Chill several hours. In a large bowl, beat egg whites and salt until almost stiff. Stir into chilled egg-liquor mixture. Slowly add milk. Fold in whipped cream and chill 1 hour. Stir and serve topped with a sprinkling of nutmeg.

Mulled Wine

A spiced warm brew with just the right touch of citrus. Drink it in front of the fire with your true love.

4" stick cinnamon
1 fifth burgundy **or** claret
1 cup boiling water
½ cup sugar

1 lemon, thinly sliced
½ orange, thinly sliced
10 whole allspice
10 whole cloves

In a large saucepan, combine water, sugar, lemon, orange, allspice and whole cloves. Bring to a boil and simmer 5 minutes. Add wine and heat just to boiling; simmer 10 minutes, being careful not to boil wine. Pour hot wine into warm mugs. Garnish each with a lemon or orange slice.

Tip: To make sure glass mugs do not break with hot liquid, place a metal spoon in mug and pour hot liquid over spoon.

Hot Buttered Rum Mix

Keep this handy mixture in the freezer for delightful winter warm-ups.

1 lb. butter, room temperature
1 lb. powdered sugar
1 lb. brown sugar

1 qt. vanilla ice cream, softened
2 tsp. nutmeg
2 tsp. cinnamon

In a large bowl, mix butter and sugars until well blended. Stir in softened ice cream and spices, blending until mixture is smooth. Place in a freezer container and seal well. This mixture will keep in the freezer for several months. To serve: mix 1-2 tbs. mix with 1 jigger of rum, bourbon or brandy in a cup or mug. Add 6 ozs. boiling water. Top with whipped cream and garnish with nutmeg or shaved chocolate if desired.

Tip: For easy shaved chocolate, use a vegetable peeler along the edge of a bitter-sweet chocolate candy bar.

Brazilian Coffee

4 cups

Here's another warm drink your man will enjoy on a cold night.

1 cup strong coffee
¼ cup semi-sweet chocolate chips
⅛ tsp. salt (optional)

3 cups milk
cinnamon sticks

In a 2-quart saucepan, melt chocolate in coffee over low heat. Add salt and gradually add milk, stirring constantly. Heat until drinking temperature. Then beat with a rotary beater until foamy. Serve in warm mugs with cinnamon sticks.

Spiced Lemon-Orange Cooler

4 cups

Here's a delightful man-pleaser for warm summer days or a pep-me-up after a workout.

1 (8 ozs.) container lemon yogurt
1 (6 ozs.) can frozen orange juice concentrate
1 tsp. vanilla

⅛ tsp. cinnamon
2 cups milk, very cold

In a blender or using a rotary beater, blend yogurt, orange juice concentrate and cinnamon until mixed.

Citrus-Yogurt Cooler

Serves 1

This drink will make him happy on a hot day, and it's good for him too!

1 cup yogurt
1 cup lime sherbet

lemon slices for garnish

In a blender, combine yogurt and lime sherbet. Pour into chilled glasses and garnish with lemon slices.

Variation: Try other flavors of yogurt and sherbet.

Dessert Coffee

One delicious way to finish a romantic dinner.

4 cups hot coffee
½ pint whipping cream
½ cup coffee-flavored liqueur
2 tbs. unsweetened cocoa powder
2 tbs. sugar
ground cinnamon

In a blender, combine ingredients. Cover and blend 30 seconds. Reheat briefly in a microwave, sprinkle with cinnamon and serve.

Sangria

Serves: 4

Curt says this is a great drink when you want to serve something different at your next barbecue. It is also great with nachos or chicken wings. It isn't necessary to buy the most expensive wine to make a good sangria.

1 (750 ml) bottle dry red wine
1 (7 ozs.) bottle club soda
juice of 1 lemon
juice of 1 orange
2 tbs. sugar
2 tbs. brandy
1 lemon, thinly sliced
1 orange, thinly sliced
1 peach, thinly sliced

Put a tray of ice cubes in a large pitcher or bowl. Add lemon and orange juice, sugar, brandy and sliced fruit. When you are ready to serve, pour in red wine and club soda. Mix well. Pour or ladle into tall glasses, making sure each glass gets a couple of ice cubes and 1-2 slices of fruit.

Charles ▶
Instant Cream Cheese Spreads (page 7)

Salads

Men love salads, especially the hearty, zesty ones. Caesar salad tops the list, followed closely by spinach salad, pasta salad and potato salad. Here are some of men's favorites.

◀ John
Not so Macho Nachos (page 14)

Classic Spinach and Bacon Salad

Serves 4-6

Spinach and bacon salad ranks almost as high as Caesar salad where men are concerned. Here is a particularly good version from John.

2 bunches spinach, stemmed
2 eggs, hard-boiled, coarsely chopped
4-6 slices bacon
8 green onions, thinly sliced
4 tbs. bacon fat
2 tbs. salad oil

1 tbs. lemon juice
2 tbs. white wine vinegar
½ tsp. sugar
freshly ground pepper
4-6 large mushrooms, thinly sliced

Tear spinach leaves into bite-sized pieces. You want about 4 ozs. or one large handful for each serving. Place spinach in a large bowl with chopped eggs. Cook bacon in a skillet until crisp, drain on paper towels, crumble and add to spinach. Remove all but 4 tbs. bacon fat from skillet. Add green onions, salad oil, lemon juice, white wine vinegar, sugar and pepper to skillet. Sauté for 1-2 minutes until onion is soft. Add sliced mushrooms and stir to coat with dressing. Remove from heat and pour over spinach, eggs and bacon. Quickly toss with hot dressing and serve.

Celery Root Salad

Serves 6-8

Chef Horst Mager created this variation of a Waldorf salad, and it's a big hit with men . . . and even women.

2 cups celery root, cut into thin matchsticks
2 cups green apples, cut into thin matchsticks
4 tbs. lemon juice
½ cup walnuts or almonds, chopped

salt and white pepper
⅓-½ cup mayonnaise
walnut halves for garnish

In a large bowl, mix all ingredients well until all celery root and apple are well coated with mayonnaise. Serve on a bed of butter lettuce, garnished with walnut halves.

Italian Gorgonzola Pasta Salad

Pasta salad is "hot," the surveys showed us. Here's a house specialty from Woodstock Wine and Deli that's a hit all year round.

Dressing:
¼ cup olive oil
¼ cup salad oil
1 tbs. Italian seasoning
2 tbs. garlic granules
4 tbs. Gorgonzola cheese
¼ cup half-and-half
2-3 tbs. lemon juice

In a mixing bowl, blender or food processor, mix olive oil, salad oil, Italian seasoning, garlic granules and Gorgonzola cheese until well blended and cheese is evenly mixed. Add half-and-half and lemon juice. Set aside.

Salad:
12 ozs. (dry weight) noodles (rigatoni), cooked, cooled
2 tbs. salad oil
½ medium red onion, chopped
4 tbs. green pepper, chopped
4-5 sun-dried tomatoes, chopped
6 ozs. Italian salami, cut into thin strips
½ cup Parmesan cheese, grated
salt and freshly ground pepper

Add oil to noodles to coat. Add onion, pepper, sun-dried tomatoes, salami and Parmesan cheese. Toss together. Add dressing and toss gently until all noodles are well coated. Add salt and pepper to taste.

Red Pepper Pesto Salad

It doesn't get better than this. Beef, pasta, good health (this recipe from the American Heart Association is 497 calories per serving), zesty spices . . . Belissimo!

2 cups cooked lean roast beef, thinly sliced, cut into 2" strips
2 tsp. garlic, minced
1½ tsp. red chili peppers, crushed
¼ cup olive oil
1 medium red bell pepper, sliced
4 ozs. pesto
salt
1 (9 ozs.) pkg. fresh angel hair pasta **or** 6 ozs. dry, cooked and drained
fresh basil sprigs (optional)

In a medium skillet, sauté garlic and crushed red chili peppers in hot olive oil to brown garlic. Add beef and red pepper strips. Sauté briefly to cook peppers and heat beef. Stir in pesto sauce. Sprinkle lightly with salt. Toss hot cooked pasta with beef-pesto mixture. Garnish each serving with a sprig of basil if desired.

French Dressing

Rudolph says he's been using this easy and delicious recipe for 50 years!

1 (10 ozs.) can tomato soup
½ cup sugar
1 tsp. salt
½ tsp. pepper
½ tsp. paprika
1 tsp. dry mustard

1 tsp. celery seed
1 tbs. Worcestershire sauce
1 medium onion, minced
¾ cup vinegar
1½ cups vegetable oil

In a blender or in a mixing bowl using a wire whisk, thoroughly blend all ingredients. Pour into a glass jar or bottle with a tight lid and refrigerate.

Layered Spinach Salad

Serves 10-12

This spinach variation of a favorite layered salad will disappear in a hurry!

1 bunch fresh spinach leaves, stems removed
½ large head iceberg lettuce, torn into bite-sized pieces
½ cup celery, chopped
8-10 green onions, white and green parts, chopped
1 green pepper, chopped
6 hard-boiled eggs, chopped
1 (10 ozs.) pkg. frozen baby peas
1 cup Parmesan cheese, grated
1 cup mayonnaise
2 tsp. sugar
8 slices bacon, fried, crumbled
1 cup Monterey Jack cheese, shredded

In a large bowl (glass will show off the layers), layer spinach, lettuce, celery, green onions, green pepper, eggs and baby peas. Sprinkle 2 tbs. Parmesan cheese over each layer. Mix mayonnaise with sugar and spread over the top. Sprinkle bacon, remaining Parmesan cheese and Monterey Jack cheese over all. Cover with plastic wrap and refrigerate at least 8 hours. Cut into wedges to serve, or toss.

Blue Cheese Dressing

2¼ cups

This is another frequently mentioned dressing in the surveys.

1 cup mayonnaise
1 cup plain yogurt
½ cup crumbled blue cheese (2 ozs.)

In a small bowl, mix mayonnaise and yogurt. Carefully stir in blue cheese.

Fantastic Greek Spinach Salad

Serves 6-8

Men clearly like salads, according to our survey. Spinach salad was one frequently mentioned, and Tom sent in his delicious Mediterranean-style creation.

2 bunches spinach, stemmed
1 medium head iceberg lettuce, torn into bite-sized pieces
⅓ cup full-flavored olive oil
1 tbs. vinegar
1 tbs. lemon juice
¾ tsp. salt
¼ tsp. dry mustard
¼ tsp. oregano
freshly ground black pepper
3 hard-boiled eggs, cut into wedges
3 medium tomatoes, cut into wedges
½ cup black olives, sliced
¼ cup feta cheese, cut into ⅜" dice

Tear spinach and lettuce leaves into a large, well chilled salad bowl. In a jar with a lid or in a blender, mix oil, vinegar, lemon juice, salt, mustard, oregano and pepper. Blend well. Arrange egg wedges and tomato wedges around edge of bowl. Sprinkle olives over all and place diced cheese in center. Pour dressing over salad and toss at the table; serve on chilled plates.

Broccoli Orange Salad

Nick enjoys making vegetable salads and this is one he particularly likes with bits of ham and some pine nuts for crunch.

1-1¼ lbs. broccoli (1 medium bunch)
2 green onions, minced
3 ozs. ham, cubed or slivered
⅓ cup mayonnaise
1 tsp. orange rind, grated
2 tbs. orange juice
dash red pepper flakes
salt and white pepper
2 tbs. pine nuts **or** sunflower seeds

Cut the bottom 2" off broccoli stem and discard. Cut flowerettes into similar sized pieces and trim about ⅛" of outside layer of broccoli stem. Cut trimmed stem into ½" rounds. Cook broccoli flowerettes and stems in boiling water for about 5 minutes. Drain, rinse well with cold water to stop cooking and place on a plate lined with paper towels. Combine mayonnaise, orange rind, orange juice, red pepper flakes, salt and white pepper. Place broccoli in a bowl, add green onions and ham, and pour dressing over broccoli. Gently mix until broccoli is well coated. Sprinkle with pine nuts before serving.

Caesar Salad

This is the salad that topped the list. For a casual evening with that special hunk, cut this recipe in half and eat the crisp leaves with your fingers.

1 large head romaine lettuce
3-4 thick slices bread, crusts removed
¼ cup olive oil
4 cloves garlic, smashed
1 egg
¼ cup lemon juice
⅓ cup olive oil
1 tsp. anchovy paste
freshly ground pepper
½ cup Parmesan cheese, freshly grated

Wash lettuce leaves, leaving them whole, and dry thoroughly. Wrap in a dish towel and refrigerate until ready to serve. Cut bread into croutons about 1" square. Heat olive oil and garlic in a large skillet and sauté croutons until crisp and brown. Discard garlic cloves. Bring a small pan of water to a rolling boil, turn down heat and place egg in water, cooking for 1-2 minutes; remove egg. Combine lemon juice, olive oil and anchovy paste with coddled egg. Beat well with a fork to form an emulsion. Place dried lettuce leaves in a large pan or bowl and toss with dressing. Arrange 4-5 lettuce leaves on each large salad plate, add freshly ground black pepper and grate 2-3 tbs. Parmesan cheese over each serving. Top with croutons.

Spicy Noodle Salad

Another category that showed up frequently in our survey was "hot and spicy." Use fresh thin Japanese or Chinese style noodles that can be found in the produce section of many supermarkets. Substitute spaghetti or linguine if they are not available. This keeps well in the 'fridge for several days.

8 ozs. fresh thin Oriental style noodles **or** 6 ozs. dry noodles, cooked
2 tbs. vegetable oil
2 ozs. bacon **or** ham
2 tbs. red wine vinegar
1 tbs. soy sauce
2 cloves garlic, minced
½ tsp. red pepper flakes
3 green onions
1 large carrot, peeled
1 tsp. sesame oil

Cook noodles as directed on package, about 1-3 minutes. Drain and rinse with cold water. Pat dry with paper towels and place in a medium bowl. Toss with vegetable oil to keep noodles from sticking together. Sauté bacon until crisp and crumble into small pieces. If using ham, cut into ¼" pieces. Combine red wine vinegar, sesame oil, soy sauce, garlic and red pepper in a small saucepan. Bring to a boil and cook 2 minutes over medium heat. Cut white parts of green onions into long slivers. Coarsely grate carrot or cut into fine strips the same size as onion. Combine noodles, bacon, vinegar sauce, sesame oil, green onions and carrot. Gently toss with two forks. Serve slightly chilled or at room temperature.

Variation: Use small salad shrimp in place of bacon or ham and substitute rice wine or cider vinegar for red wine vinegar.

Italian Bean and Tuna Salad

Here's another man-pleaser. This salad is great on its own for lunch, or serve it as part of a party antipasto platter with salami slices, black olives, spicy peppers, radishes and cheese cubes.

1 (15 ozs.) can cannellini **or** garbanzo beans
1 (6½ ozs.) can tuna, well drained
2 tbs. celery, finely diced
2 tbs. red onion, finely diced
2 tbs. Italian parsley, minced
1 small clove garlic, minced
2 tbs. full-flavored olive oil
2 tbs. red wine vinegar
1 tbs. lemon juice
dash Tabasco
salt and freshly ground pepper
chopped tomato or roasted red
   pepper strips for garnish

Place beans in a sieve, rinse briefly under running water and drain. Place remaining ingredients in a bowl and stir with a fork to break up tuna pieces. Add beans and mix gently. Refrigerate for 1-2 hours before serving. Garnish with chopped tomato pieces or red pepper strips.

Cobb Salad

This is a chef's salad with great style and substance. It makes a terrific patio lunch or supper. Serve with some crisp breadsticks or garlic bread.

1 head romaine lettuce
1 head butter lettuce **or** red leaf lettuce
½ lb. bacon, cooked crisp, crumbled
2-3 ripe tomatoes, peeled, seeded, cut into large pieces
2 cups cooked chicken **or** turkey, cut into ¾" pieces
⅓ lb. blue **or** Roquefort cheese, crumbled
2 ripe avocados, peeled, cut into ½" pieces

Dressing:
⅓ cup full-flavored olive oil
2 tbs. white wine vinegar
1 tsp. Dijon mustard
1 garlic clove, finely minced
1 tbs. parsley, finely chopped
¼ tsp. sugar
freshly ground pepper

Combine dressing ingredients and mix well. Tear lettuce into bite-sized pieces, place in a salad bowl and toss with all but 3 tbs. dressing. Arrange bacon, tomatoes, chicken, cheese and avocado pieces in rows on top of dressed greens. Drizzle with remaining dressing and serve.

Old-Fashioned Potato Salad

Bob's grandmother taught him how to make this salad. He still remembers how good the house smelled with cooking potatoes when he came home from school. He suggests making this a day ahead so the flavors have a chance to blend.

2 lbs. boiling potatoes, peeled, cooked
3 eggs, hard-boiled
½ cup mayonnaise
½ cup sour cream
2 tbs. Dijon mustard
⅓ cup sweet pickles, finely chopped
⅓ cup sweet white onion, finely chopped
⅓ cup parsley, minced
salt and freshly ground pepper
paprika for garnish

Cut cooked potatoes into 1″ cubes and run eggs through egg slicer twice or chop coarsely. Place in a large bowl, add mayonnaise, sour cream, mustard, pickles, onion, parsley, salt and pepper. Mix gently until well combined (hands work well for this). Sprinkle top of salad with a little paprika. Cover and refrigerate until ready to serve. Makes about 1 quart.

Sam's Shrimp Louie

Sam says a little of this dressing can be used on shrimp or crab without the lettuce and is a nice change from the usual red cocktail sauce. Make it easy on yourself and buy the large cooked salad shrimp from the fish market for this salad.

Dressing:
1 cup mayonnaise
¼ cup prepared chili sauce
2 tbs. white onion, minced or grated
1 tsp. Worcestershire sauce
1 tsp. lemon juice
dash Tabasco
2 tbs. milk **or** light cream
salt and white pepper
1 tsp. brandy (optional)

1 large head butter lettuce **or** red lettuce
1 lb. shrimp, peeled, deveined, cooked
2 ripe tomatoes, cut into quarters
2 eggs, hard-boiled, cut into quarters
10-12 black olives

Combine dressing ingredients, mix well and refrigerate until ready to use. This can be done a day ahead if you like. Tear lettuce into bite-sized pieces and place on 4 serving plates. Mix shrimp with dressing and place in the center of each plate. Garnish with tomato, egg wedges and black olives. Serve with French bread and a sauvignon blanc wine.

Ken's Macaroni Salad

Men tell us that macaroni salads are high on their list and this version is sure to please. Make it several hours or a day ahead and let it mellow in the refrigerator before serving.

1 cup uncooked salad macaroni
2 hard-boiled eggs, chopped
1 tbs. green onion, minced
¼ cup sweet pickle, finely chopped
¼ cup celery, finely chopped
1 tbs. capers
1 cup green peas, cooked
2 tbs. pimiento, chopped

½ cup mayonnaise
2 tbs. pickle juice
1 tsp. Dijon mustard
¼ tsp. white pepper
1 tsp. salt
2 tbs. sour cream
2 tbs. parsley, minced

Cook macaroni in boiling water for 12 minutes, or according to package directions. Drain and rinse with cold water. Drain well. Place in a mixing bowl and add chopped eggs, onion, pickle, celery, capers, peas and pimiento. Combine mayonnaise, pickle juice, mustard, pepper, salt and sour cream. Add to macaroni with parsley. Toss lightly with two forks. Chill before serving.

Zesty "One Shot" Italian Dressing

2 cups

Warren was a restauranteur and developed this recipe out of items he said were readily available in his cupboard. Guests asked him for this recipe more than any other.

½ cup catsup
½ cup salad oil
½ cup wine vinegar
1 clove garlic, chopped
⅓ cup onion, chopped
½ tsp. salt

1 tsp. Dijon mustard
1 tsp. paprika
1 tsp. Worcestershire sauce
2 tsp. sugar
½ cup fresh parsley, chopped **or** 2 tbs. dried

Blend all ingredients in a blender; store in the refrigerator in a jar or bottle with a tight fitting lid.

Chinese Chicken Salad

Crunchy lettuce, peanuts and a mildly spicy dressing combined with some cooked chicken or turkey make a great lunch with your "significant other."

2 cups chicken, shredded or thinly sliced **or** turkey
2 tbs. soy sauce
2 tbs. rice wine vinegar
2 tbs. peanut oil
1 tsp. sesame oil
2 tsp. Dijon mustard
dash red pepper flakes
½ tsp. sugar
salt and freshly ground pepper
2-3 cups iceberg lettuce, shredded
1 cup carrots, coarsely grated
4 green onions, thinly sliced
¼ cup dry roasted unsalted peanuts, chopped
fresh cilantro leaves for garnish

Combine shredded chicken, soy sauce, rice wine vinegar, peanut oil, sesame oil, mustard, red pepper flakes, sugar, salt and pepper in a medium bowl. Marinate in the refrigerator while preparing remaining ingredients, or for several hours. To assemble: shred lettuce and carrots and place on individual plates or a platter. Sprinkle with green onion slices. Drizzle marinade from chicken over lettuce and carrots. Mound chicken in the center and garnish with peanuts and fresh cilantro leaves.

South-of-the-Border Salad

This hearty salad features red kidney beans, yellow corn, green chilies and cumin. It's wonderful with grilled steaks or chicken.

4 ozs. small pasta shells, uncooked
1 (15 ozs.) can red kidney beans, well drained
1 (12 ozs.) can whole kernel corn, well drained
4-5 green onions, finely chopped
4-5 tbs. canned green chilies, finely chopped
½ cup cheddar cheese, diced into ½" pieces
½ tsp. ground cumin
1 tsp. dried oregano
1 tbs. lemon juice
½ cup mayonnaise
salt and freshly ground pepper

Cook pasta according to package directions. Drain and immediately rinse with cold water. Drain well and set aside. Rinse kidney beans and corn under cold water and drain well. Combine pasta with remaining ingredients and gently toss with two forks. Chill in refrigerator for at least two hours before serving. Add a little more mayonnaise if salad seems dry.

Artichoke and Garbanzo Bean Salad

Serves 4

This quick salad features some wonderful Greek flavors. It isn't fragile, so you and he can take it along on your next backpack or bicycle outing.

1 (6½ ozs.) jar marinated artichoke crowns, drained, cut
  into ¾" chunks, liquid reserved
1 (15 ozs.) can garbanzo beans, drained, rinsed with cold water
4-5 sun-dried tomatoes (packed in oil), cut into slivers
3 ozs. feta cheese, diced or crumbled
2 green onions, thinly sliced
2 tbs. parsley, minced
¼ tsp. dried oregano
2 tbs. artichoke liquid
1 tbs. white wine vinegar
1 tbs. lemon juice
salt and freshly ground pepper
8-10 black Greek olives

Combine all ingredients. Cover and refrigerate for 1-2 hours or overnight before serving. If you like, add some slivers of salami or ham chunks for a real main dish salad.

Deli Pasta Salad

This salad takes on a new look just by changing the deli meats and cheese. Serve it in radiccio or lettuce cups placed on a platter for a barbecue, or as a first course for a small dinner party.

8 ozs. egg noodles, uncooked
3 ozs. mortadella, **or** ham or bologna, thinly sliced
3 ozs. Gruyere **or** Swiss cheese, thinly sliced
1 large dill pickle
1 large or 2 small tart green apples, peeled
1½ tbs. Worcestershire sauce
1 tbs. Dijon mustard
3-4 tbs. mayonnaise
½ cup sour cream
½ tsp. white pepper
2 tbs. Parmesan cheese, freshly grated
2 tbs. parsley, minced

Cook noodles according to package directions. Immediately drain, rinse with cold water and drain again. Cut meat, cheese and pickle into strips about the same width and thickness as noodles. Coarsely grate apple. Combine noodles with meat, cheese, apple and pickle. Add Worcestershire sauce, mustard, mayonnaise, sour cream, white pepper and grated cheese. Gently toss with two forks until well mixed. Refrigerate for at least two hours or overnight before serving. Garnish with minced parsley.

Meat and More Meat

Beef is men's food! Beef finished far ahead of pork and lamb as far as the men in our surveys were concerned. (In fact, in the case of lamb, they either liked it a great deal or it appeared on their "Foods You Dislike" list.) They liked beef grilled, or spiced up in casseroles, chili and stews. A lot of men are also doing more stir-frying, and we're including their creative recipes. They contributed some terrific pork recipes, sausage dishes, a great barbecued leg of lamb, and hundreds of good ideas. Here are some of the best.

Steaks, Steaks and Steaks!

There are several small things you can do to assure that the expensive steak you bring home is cooked perfectly. Always have the meat at room temperature when you put it on the fire. This allows the middle to be cooked to the desired doneness without drying out the surface. The surface of the meat should be dry when it is put on the fire. This allows a crust to form and limits moisture loss, making for a juicier, more tender steak. Don't salt a steak before cooking. You will draw the moisture from the meat. Instead, let everyone salt to their own taste at the table. Trim steak of all but ¼" of fat. Leaving more fat will cause flare-ups on the barbecue or oven broiler. Turn the steak with tongs, not a fork, which punctures the surface and allows the juices to escape. Turn the steak only once during cooking.

Barbecuing on a Gas Fired Broiler

Be sure to preheat the grill according to manufacturer directions. If grates are adjustable, set them as close to the flame as possible.

Barbecuing Over Coals

Use a good grade of hardwood briquettes or better yet, charcoal. Start the fire with an electrical starter, not lighter fluid which always leaves a slight taste. Start out with plenty of charcoal, and start early enough so that the coals burn down to nice even heat.

Broiling in the Oven

Many oven broilers do not get hot enough to properly broil a steak. Be sure to preheat the broiler and pan for several minutes. Place the broiler pan as close to the heat as possible.

Cast Iron Pan Broiled Steaks

Be sure your meat is trimmed of all fat and at room temperature. Pat with paper towels to dry. Heat a 10" heavy cast iron skillet over high heat until very hot (2-3 minutes). Put steaks in skillet, pressing down with spatula or your hand to make sure meat has good contact with skillet. Cook 1" steaks 3-4 minutes each side for medium rare, longer for well done.

Variations:
- Rub broiled steak with a cut garlic clove.
- Top broiled steak with sautéed mushrooms.
- Top broiled steak with sautéed onions.
- Top broiled steak with Gorganzola or Roquefort topping: blend ¼ cup cheese with 2 tbs. cream.

Wine Sauce for Steak

Serves 2-3

2 tbs. butter
¼ lb. fresh mushrooms, sliced
2 tbs. flour

½ cup red wine
1 cup beef stock

In a skillet, melt butter and sauté mushrooms until almost tender. Blend in flour. Add wine and beef stock. Stir until smooth and gently simmer for 2-3 minutes.

Teriyaki Beef Stir-Fry

Serves 4

Here is another winner from the American Heart Association. Even if he's on a diet, he can enjoy this tasty medley of flavors for 247 delicious calories. He'll love you for it!

1 lb. beef top round, cut into thin strips
3 tbs. teriyaki sauce
2 tbs. oil, divided
2 tsp. cornstarch
2 red, yellow or green bell peppers, cut into ¾" cubes
6 green onions, cut into 2" slices

In a shallow glass bowl, combine teriyaki sauce, 1 tbs. oil and cornstarch. Add beef strips and marinate 30 minutes. In a frying pan or wok, stir-fry bell peppers and green onions in 1 tbs. oil about 3 minutes; remove from pan. Stir-fry beef 2-3 minutes. Return vegetables to pan; cook until hot. Serve with rice.

Sweet and Sour Beef and Cabbage

Serves 4-6

Bob developed this recipe because he thought it had the flavor of cabbage rolls with less work. He guarantees that even people who don't like cabbage love this dish.

Sauce:
2 (8 ozs. each) cans tomato sauce
¼ cup cider vinegar
¼ cup brown sugar
½ tsp. salt
¼ tsp. pepper

In a small bowl, combine tomato sauce, vinegar, sugar, salt and pepper. Set aside.

1 lb. lean ground beef
½ cup soft bread crumbs
1 egg, slightly beaten
½ medium onion, finely chopped
½ green pepper, seeded, chopped
1 clove garlic, minced
2 tbs. parsley, chopped
1 tsp. salt
2 tbs. salad oil
1 head cabbage (about 2 lbs.)

In a mixing bowl, combine ground beef, bread crumbs, egg, onion, green pepper, garlic, parsley and salt. Mix with hands until well blended and shape into balls the size of golf balls. In a large Dutch oven, heat oil and brown meat balls, turning to brown evenly on all sides. Drain off any fat. Remove core from cabbage and cut cabbage into narrow wedges; arrange them over meat. Pour sweet and sour sauce over cabbage and meat. Cover pan and reduce heat. Simmer gently for 15-30 minutes or until cabbage is tender.

Fire Brigade Chili

*This is a prize-winning recipe from the Great Chili Cook-off. Fair warning: this is for the man who really loves **hot** chili. Tone down the spices for a milder dish.*

3 lbs. beef chuck, diced
3 cups water
1 cup beef broth
1 (8 ozs.) can tomato sauce
6 tbs. garlic powder
¼ cup hot chili powder
¼ cup mild chili powder
3 tbs. cumin
3 tbs. onion, minced
2 tbs. paprika
3 tbs. ground red pepper
1 tbs. sugar
2 tsp. salt
chopped tomato, chopped green onion, shredded cheddar cheese and
    a dollop of sour cream for garnish

In a large skillet, brown meat over high heat in 3 batches, transferring to a Dutch oven with a slotted spoon. Add remaining ingredients, water, broth, tomato sauce, garlic powder, chili powders, cumin, minced onion, paprika, ground red pepper, sugar and salt. Bring to a boil; reduce heat and simmer uncovered, stirring occasionally, 1½-3 hours. Garnish with chopped tomato, green onion, shredded cheddar cheese and a spoonful of sour cream.

Quick Beef Stroganoff

Serves 4-5

Here is a savory dish from Dennis' recipe files.

1 medium onion, chopped
½ lb. fresh mushrooms, sliced
5 tbs. butter **or** margarine
½ cup dry sherry
16-20 ozs. sirloin steak,
  sliced into thin strips

1 (10¾ ozs.) can tomato soup
1 (10¾ ozs.) beef broth
1 pt. sour cream
salt and freshly ground pepper
chopped fresh parsley **or** parsley
  flakes for garnish

In a large frying pan, sauté mushrooms and onions in butter or margarine until onions are translucent. Add sherry. Add steak and cook until browned. Add tomato soup and beef broth and simmer, covered on low heat for 1 hour. Add sour cream and serve over noodles. Sprinkle with parsley.

Favorite Beef Stew

Serves 4-5

Charles recommends this recipe because it is delicious and so easy to bake in the oven.

1½ lean beef cubes
3 tbs. oil
flour seasoned with salt and pepper
2 medium onions, sliced
2 cloves garlic, minced
4-5 carrots, sliced
3-4 celery stalks, cut into 2" pieces

½ medium green pepper,
  sliced into rings
4 potatoes, peeled, thickly sliced
½ tsp. thyme
salt and freshly ground black pepper
½ cup tomato juice

Dredge beef cubes in flour seasoned with salt and pepper. Heat oil in a heavy skillet and brown beef cubes on all sides. Remove meat and place in a casserole. Add onions, garlic, carrots, celery and green pepper to skillet and sauté for 3-4 minutes, scraping up brown bits. Add potatoes and carrot-onion mixture to casserole, season with salt, pepper and thyme and pour in tomato juice. Cover tightly and bake in a 350° oven for about 1¾ hours or until meat is very tender.

James ▶
Citrus-Yogurt Cooler (page 19)

Enchiladas Olé

This is Art's favorite recipe to prepare for family and guests.

2 tbs. oil
1 lb. lean ground beef
½ cup onions, chopped
1 clove garlic, minced
⅓ cup prepared salsa **or** Mexican style hot sauce
2 (8 ozs. each) cans tomato sauce
2 tsp. cumin
2 tsp. chili powder
1 lb. Monterey Jack cheese, grated
¼ cup oil
1 pkg. corn tortillas (12)
¼ cup onions, chopped
black olives, sliced for garnish

Brown meat and onions in oil, breaking up meat with a spatula. Add garlic, 2 tbs. salsa, 1 can tomato sauce, cumin and chili powder. Simmer over low heat for 15-20 minutes. Combine remaining salsa and tomato sauce and set aside. Soften tortillas by frying in oil 5 seconds each side; drain on paper towels. Fill tortillas with meat mixture and some grated cheese and roll up. Place tortillas seam side down in a lightly greased 9" x 12" pan; top with remaining sauce, cheese and onions. Bake at 350° for 15 minutes. Garnish with black olives.

◄ **Bill**
Fantastic Greek Spinach Salad (page 28)

Kenneth's Italiana Meat Loaf

Serves 2-3

He spices up his meat loaf with some hot Italian sausage. It's fast, too — bakes in less than an hour.

2 tbs. full-flavored olive oil
¼ cup fresh mushrooms, chopped
¼ cup onions, chopped
3 cloves garlic, chopped
2 tbs. green peppers, chopped
2 tbs. celery, chopped
¾ lb. lean ground chuck
2 hot Italian sausages, skin removed, crumbled
1 egg
3 ozs. dry vermouth
¼ cup seasoned Italian bread crumbs
¼ tsp. Italian seasoning
¼ tsp. salt
dash oregano
¼ cup Parmesan cheese

Preheat oven to 350°. Sauté mushrooms, onions, garlic, green peppers and celery in olive oil until softened. Place ground chuck and sausages in a mixing bowl. Beat egg with vermouth and add to meat. Stir in bread crumbs, Italian seasoning, salt, oregano and cooked vegetable mixture. Place in a loaf pan and bake at 350° for 45 minutes. Sprinkle Parmesan cheese over loaf, return to oven and bake an additional 5 minutes.

Greek Style Stuffed Green Peppers

Serves 6

This is John's specialty. He says to serve it with garlic bread, wine, and a gleam in your eye.

1 lb. lean hamburger
1 medium onion, diced
1 tsp. cinnamon
2 tsp. oregano
½ tsp. **each** salt and pepper
2 (8 ozs. each) cans tomato sauce
½ cup red wine
1 clove garlic, finely diced
½ cup long grain rice, uncooked
6 green peppers
butter to taste

Brown hamburger in a skillet. Drain off fat and add onions, cinnamon, oregano, salt, pepper, tomato sauce, red wine and garlic. Bring to a boil, add rice and simmer covered over low heat for about 40 minutes until rice is tender. Cut off pepper tops and reserve. Clean out seeds and set peppers in a baking dish with ¼ cup of water in bottom of dish. Dish should be as deep as the peppers. Stuff peppers with cooked meat mixture, add a small piece of butter to each and replace pepper tops. Bake at 350° for 1 hour or until fork penetrates pepper easily.

Jim's Western Barbecue

Jim has been serving this delicious steak to guests for nearly 20 years, and they always ask for his recipe. He recommends completing the menu with rice pilaf or small red potatoes and a Caesar salad.

3 lbs. top round steak, cut 1½" thick
meat tenderizer
4-5 slices bacon
½ cup green onions, chopped
1 large clove garlic, minced
¼ cup wine vinegar
1 tbs. Worcestershire sauce
1 cup water
1 cup catsup
¼ cup molasses
2 tsp. dry mustard
⅛ tsp. Tabasco

Sprinkle both sides of meat with tenderizer and pierce with a fork. Cover loosely and refrigerate overnight. Cook bacon until crisp. Remove from pan and drain all but 1 tbs. fat. Sauté onions and garlic until onion is translucent. Add wine vinegar, Worcestershire sauce, water, catsup, molasses, dry mustard and Tabasco. Brush meat with sauce and place on rack over hot coals, 4-6" from coals. Cook 6-8 minutes each side for medium rare meat. Turn only once. Baste frequently with sauce as meat cooks. Do not overcook. (Tenderizing cuts cooking time.) Carve meat at an angle across the grain in thin slices. Serve with remaining sauce.

Variation: Try the sauce on hamburgers.

Beefball Supreme

This is one of Rick's favorite recipes. The special woman in his life cooks it for him with great results. Great results! Try it!

1 lb. ground beef
salt and freshly ground pepper
½ cup fine dry bread crumbs
½ cup milk
4 tbs. oil
1 tsp. Worcestershire sauce
1 small onion, chopped
½ lb. mushrooms, sliced
2 tbs. flour
1 cup beef bouillon
¼ cup sour cream

In a medium bowl, place beef; add salt, pepper, milk and bread crumbs and gently combine. Form into 1" balls. In a medium skillet, brown beef balls in 3 tbs. oil. Remove from skillet and set aside. Add remaining oil to skillet; sauté onions and mushrooms until onion is translucent and mushrooms are tender, about 10 minutes. Sprinkle flour over vegetables, stirring to blend. Gradually add bouillon, stirring constantly. Return meatballs to skillet and add Worcestershire sauce. Cover and simmer 20 minutes. Just before serving, stir in sour cream. Serve over steamed rice.

Baked Brisket

This goes in the oven, bakes for 3-4 hours and melts in his mouth. It is terrific for sandwiches, too.

3-4 lbs. boneless beef (not corned) brisket, exterior fat trimmed
1 large onion, thinly sliced
2 cloves garlic, thinly sliced
1 cup catsup
½ cup beef broth
2 tbs. cider vinegar
1 tbs. creamy horseradish
1 tbs. whole grain mustard **or** Dijon mustard
salt and freshly ground pepper

Place brisket in a baking pan or casserole just large enough to hold meat. Top with onion and garlic slices. Mix remaining ingredients together in a small bowl and pour over brisket. Cover tightly with lid or foil and bake at 300° for 3-4 hours until tender. Remove from oven, slice thinly and serve with some of the sauce over rice or potatoes; or allow to cool and refrigerate overnight. Lift off hardened fat. Reheat in a little of the sauce, or slice thin for sandwiches.

Japanese Style Grilled Flank Steak

Serves 4

Nelson's fresh ginger and soy sauce marinade gives this steak a wonderful flavor. Don't marinate it more than 30 minutes.

1-1½ lbs. flank steak, trimmed of all fat
grated lemon peel from 1 lemon
2 tbs. fresh lemon juice
2 tbs. peanut oil

2 tbs. soy sauce
1 tsp. fresh ginger, grated
1 clove garlic, finely minced
freshly ground black pepper

Place flank steak in a flat pan with sides. Grate lemon peel over steak. Add remaining ingredients to steak in pan. Turn steak over once or twice to coat both sides with marinade. Marinate about 30 minutes. Grill on the barbecue, indoor grill, or broil in the oven 3-4 minutes a side for medium rare meat. Do not overcook; steak should remain quite rare in the middle. Remove to a cutting board and slice very thinly on the diagonal across the grain.

Surfburger

Serves 1

This terrific burger is a specialty of the Surf Restaurant. Many, many men mentioned burgers as the sandwich of choice, and many more said they loved barbecuing "gourmet" burgers.

For each burger:
⅓ lb. lean ground beef
1-2 tbs. blue cheese
dash minced dried garlic
lots of freshly ground black pepper
1 hamburger bun or French roll

Divide ground beef in half and flatten into two circles about 3½"-4" in diameter. Crumble blue cheese over the center of one patty, stopping ½" from edges. Sprinkle with minced garlic and black pepper. Top with other patty, firmly pressing outside edges together. Barbecue over a hot fire or pan grill and serve on a toasted bun or roll.

Dad's Spanish Rice

Serves 6-8

Bob's family is always asking for this dish. It is better made a day ahead and reheated.

2 cups water
¾ cup uncooked rice
1 tbs. vegetable oil
1 onion, chopped
2 lbs. ground beef
2 stalks celery, diced
2 (10 ozs. each) cans tomato soup

½ cup catsup
1 tbs. Worcestershire sauce
1 tbs. vinegar
2 tbs. sugar
1 tbs. chili powder
¼ tsp. salt

Bring water to a boil in a medium saucepan. Add rice, cover and cook over low heat about 12 minutes. Drain off excess water. While rice is cooking, heat oil in a large skillet. Sauté onion and celery until soft but not brown. Remove from skillet and set aside. Sauté ground beef in skillet, crumbling into small pieces with a spatula as it cooks. Pour off fat. Add onion, celery, drained rice, tomato soup and remaining ingredients to skillet. Cover and simmer 10-15 minutes to blend flavors, stirring as little as possible.

Horst Mager's Hungarian Goulash

The flavors of beef and pork cooked with simple spices blend into a fabulous and satisfying main dish.

1 lb. beef chuck, cut into 2" cubes
½ lb. boneless pork, cut into 2" cubes
4 tbs. flour
¼ tsp. caraway seed
salt and freshly ground pepper
4 tbs. olive oil
3 medium onions, sliced
1-2 cloves garlic, chopped
3 tbs. tomato paste
4 tbs. good quality paprika
1 qt. beef stock **or** beef broth

Pat cubed meat dry with paper towels. Mix flour, caraway seed, salt and pepper in a bag to combine. Shake meat until well coated. In a large skillet, heat olive oil and brown meat. Remove meat and set aside. In the same skillet, sauté onions and garlic until onions are translucent but garlic is not brown. Return meat to pan; add tomato paste, paprika and beef stock. Cover and simmer in a 325° oven 1½ hours, or until meat is tender. Remove from oven and allow to cool slightly so that any excess fat can be skimmed off. Serve over Poppy Seed Noodles (recipe follows) or mashed potatoes.

Poppy Seed Noodles

Cook 8 ozs. of dried egg noodles as directed on package. Drain and toss with 1 tbs. melted butter and 1 tbs. poppy seeds.

Marinated Pork Roast

Serves 8-10

This simple recipe will end up on your repeat list. Marinating the pork overnight allows the flavors to sink deep into the meat. Mashed potatoes or a rice dish and carrots are perfect accompaniments.

½ cup soy sauce
½ cup dry sherry
2 cloves garlic, minced

1 tbs. dry mustard
1 tsp. ground ginger
1 (4-5 lb.) boneless, rolled pork roast

In a small bowl, mix soy sauce, sherry, minced garlic, dry mustard and ground ginger. Place roast in a heavy plastic bag in a roasting pan. Pour marinade mixture into bag and close tightly. Press bag against meat to distribute marinade. Marinate for 2-3 hours or overnight in refrigerator. Remove meat from bag; place on a rack in a roasting pan. Bake uncovered at 350° for 2½-3 hours or until inserted thermometer registers 175°. Baste often with marinade.

Italian Sausage with Peppers and Onions

Serves 2-3

Mike's contribution is great by itself or made into a hearty sandwich. The peppers don't have to be peeled but it's a nice touch.

1 lb. Italian sausages, mild **or** hot
½ cup water
1 large green pepper

1 large red pepper
1 large yellow onion, thinly sliced
⅓ cup white wine

Place sausages in a small saucepan with ½ cup of water, cover and bring to a boil. Cook for about 5 minutes, piercing each sausage with a fork or knife point to release fat once or twice. Cut peppers into sections along their natural ridges and peel with a vegetable peeler. Cut into long strips. Pour liquid and fat from sausages; add peppers, onion and white wine to saucepan. Cover and cook over low heat for 10 minutes. Remove cover, turn up heat and brown sausages. Slice each sausage into several pieces to serve, or slice lengthwise for sandwiches.

Stuffed Pork Chops

Serves 6

Thick juicy pork chops with a succulent stuffing are something men dream about! And they dream about the cook!

4 tbs. butter
6 pork loin chops, 2" thick,
   with deeply cut pocket
1 stalk celery, finely chopped
1 medium onion, finely chopped
1 clove garlic, finely minced
¼ cup mushrooms, finely chopped
¼ cup walnuts, chopped
¼ cup apple, finely shredded
1 tsp. thyme

½ tsp. sage
1¼ cup dry whole wheat bread crumbs
¼ cup parsley, chopped
1 cup chicken broth
1 tbs. olive oil
1 tbs. butter
¼ tsp. sage
freshly ground black pepper
2-4 tbs. white wine

In a medium skillet, sauté celery, onion, garlic and mushrooms in butter until vegetables are translucent. In a medium bowl, mix walnuts, apple, thyme, sage, bread crumbs and parsley. Add sautéed vegetables and combine. Add enough chicken broth to hold stuffing together. Fill pork chop pockets with stuffing and secure with toothpicks. In a heavy skillet, brown chops well in olive oil and butter. Sprinkle with sage and black pepper. Cover bottom of a casserole with remaining chicken broth and white wine. Cover pan tightly. Bake at 350° for 1½ hours or until tender.

Baked Spareribs

Serves 4-6

Ribs are another undisputed first choice of the male species. These spareribs have a delightful sweet and sour flavor. Although they may serve 4-6, two or three men will polish them all off with ease — if you're lucky enough to eat dinner with two or three men!

3 lbs. lean spareribs, cut into serving pieces
salt and freshly ground pepper
½ cup onion, finely chopped
½ cup green pepper, chopped
1½ cups catsup **or** 1 (16 ozs.) can tomato sauce
1 tbs. Worcestershire sauce
⅓ cup vinegar
⅓ cup brown sugar
½ tsp. dry mustard
1 (8 ozs.) can pineapple tidbits with juice

Place spareribs in a shallow baking pan. Sprinkle with salt and pepper. Bake at 450° for 30 minutes; pour off all fat. While spareribs are baking, in a small bowl mix onion, green pepper, catsup, Worcestershire sauce, vinegar, brown sugar, dry mustard, pineapple and juice. Pour ½ sauce over ribs, reduce oven temperature to 350° and bake one hour, basting frequently. Pour on remaining sauce and bake 30 minutes more, basting every 10 minutes.

Chuck ▶
Fire Brigade Chili (page 45) and Beer Bread (page 145)

Joe's Jambalaya

This recipe uses sausages and ham, but Joe also likes it with chicken or shrimp.

4 slices bacon
6 link sausages
1 large onion, coarsely chopped
1 large clove garlic, minced
1 stalk celery, finely diced
1 green pepper, diced
1 cup uncooked rice
2 tbs. tomato paste
1 (14 ozs.) can chicken broth
1 (14 ozs.) can Italian style tomatoes with juice

½ tsp. thyme
½ tsp. salt
⅛ tsp. ground cloves
¼ tsp. white pepper
¼ tsp. chili powder
4-6 drops Tabasco
2 cups ham, diced
¼ cup parsley, minced

Preheat oven to 350°. Cut bacon into 1" pieces and sausages into ½" slices. Sauté together in a large ovenproof skillet until brown. Remove meat and pour off all but 2 tbs. fat. Add onion, garlic, celery and green pepper and sauté until onion is soft. Add rice and mix well. Add tomato paste, chicken broth, tomatoes with juice, thyme, salt, cloves, pepper, chili powder and Tabasco. Bring to a boil and add ham, sausage, bacon and parsley. Cover tightly and bake in a 350° oven for about 1 hour. Check from time to time to make sure there is enough liquid. Add ¼ cup water if necessary. Serve when liquid has been absorbed and rice is tender.

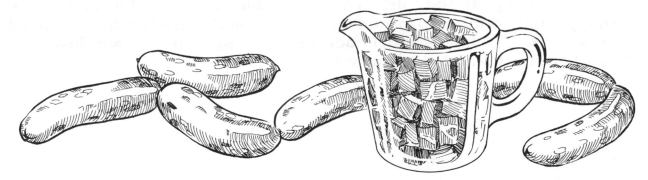

◀ **Gust**
Chicken Oriental Stir-Fry (page 85)

Spicy Pork with Noodles

If you can't find thin Japanese or Chinese fresh noodles for this dish, substitute whole wheat spaghetti.

¼ cup vegetable oil
1 lb. fresh mushrooms, sliced
1½ lbs. pork cutlets
1½ tbs. cornstarch
2 tbs. **each** soy sauce and dry sherry
3 tbs. vegetable oil
1 clove garlic, minced
6 green onions, thinly sliced
1 green pepper, coarsely chopped
½ tsp. red pepper flakes
2 cups chicken broth
1 tsp. sesame oil
1 lb. cooked Chinese noodles **or** whole wheat spaghetti
1 (10 ozs.) pkg. frozen peas, cooked

Heat ¼ cup oil in a large skillet. Sauté mushrooms 4-5 minutes. Set aside. Slice pork into ¼" x 1" matchsticks. Combine sliced pork with cornstarch, soy sauce and sherry; let stand about 15 minutes. Heat 3 tbs. oil in skillet (or wok). When very hot, add marinated pork, green onions, garlic and red pepper. Stir constantly 3-4 minutes until pork is cooked. Remove meat from skillet and pour off remaining oil. Add chicken broth to skillet, bring to a boil and scrape brown bits from bottom of pan. Add mushrooms, pork, sesame oil and cooked noodles. Cook 2-3 minutes until noodles are hot. Stir in peas. Serve in a large bowl that has been warmed in the oven.

Bob's Savory Sausage Casserole

This is Bob's favorite dish to make for the ski crowd, or to take to a potluck.

1 cup uncooked rice
1 (2 ozs.) pkg. chicken noodle soup mix
3½ cups boiling water
1 lb. bulk pork sausage
1 large onion, chopped
1 green or red pepper, chopped
2 medium stalks celery, thinly sliced
2 large tomatoes, peeled, seeded, chopped
½ tsp. salt
¼-½ cup sour cream
3 tbs. Parmesan cheese, grated
1-2 tbs. butter

Combine rice and noodle soup mix in a large saucepan with boiling water. Cover and cook over low heat 20-25 minutes until rice is tender. Stir occasionally during cooking. Brown sausage in a skillet, breaking it into small pieces with a spatula. Remove from skillet with a slotted spoon and drain on paper towels. Pour out all but 1-2 tbs. fat and add onion, pepper and celery to skillet. Sauté 4-5 minutes until vegetables are soft. Preheat oven to 375°. In a mixing bowl, combine cooked rice, sausage, vegetables, tomatoes and salt. Mix in enough sour cream to moisten. Place in an oiled casserole, sprinkle with Parmesan cheese and dot with butter. Bake at 375° for 15-20 minutes until casserole is hot and top is slightly browned.

Variations:
- Use as a stuffing for green peppers or fresh tomatoes. Parboil peppers 5 minutes before stuffing, fill with sausage mixture and bake uncovered for 20 minutes at 375°.
- Stir in a tablespoon of soy sauce and combine with 2 lightly scrambled eggs for a quick fried rice dish for breakfast or lunch.

Roasted Leg of Lamb

Those men who enjoy lamb rated roasted leg of lamb as their #1 choice. This recipe is loaded with flavorful garlic and oregano. The initial high heat seals in all the wonderful juices.

4-5 cloves of garlic
1 tbs. salt
1 tsp. pepper
4-5 lbs. leg of lamb
juice of 1 lemon
2 tsp. oregano
2 tbs. butter
1 cup hot water
1 tbs. **each** cornstarch and hot water

Peel and cut each clove of garlic in half. Sprinkle with salt and pepper. With the tip of a sharp knife, make 10 deep slits over entire leg of lamb. Insert garlic into slits. Rub lamb with lemon juice and sprinkle evenly with salt, pepper and oregano. Place on a rack in a roasting pan. Rub with butter. Pour water in bottom of pan. Bake at 400° for 25 minutes. Reduce temperature to 350° and bake for 1-1½ hours longer. A meat thermometer inserted should read 160° for medium and 170°-180° for well done. Turn roast halfway through roasting time, adding water as necessary. When done, remove roast and skim off fat. Add more water to drippings to make 1 cup. Dissolve 1 tbs. cornstarch in 1 tbs. water and add to liquid; cook, stirring, until thickened. Slice roast and serve with gravy.

Tip: Mint jelly is the perfect complement to roast lamb.

East Indian Lamb

Looking for something a little exotic for your next dinner party? Lou offers his recipe for lamb with a nut yogurt sauce to be served over rice.

2 lbs. boneless leg of lamb
¼ cup clarified butter*
1½ cups yellow onions, chopped
2 cloves garlic, minced
½ tsp. turmeric
¼ tsp. powdered cardamom
¼ tsp. cinnamon
½ tsp. freshly ground black pepper
1 tsp. salt
1 cup plain yogurt
2 cups water
½ cup ground blanched almonds
⅓ cup heavy cream
⅓ cup fresh cilantro leaves, very finely chopped
2½ cups uncooked rice, cooked

Trim fat from lamb and cut into 1" cubes. Heat clarified butter in a heavy saucepan. Add onion, sauté until golden and add garlic, turmeric, cardamom, cinnamon and black pepper. Cook for a minute and add lamb cubes. Toss gently to coat lamb with spice-onion mixture. Add salt, yogurt and water; cover pot and simmer over low heat for 45 minutes. Remove cover and increase heat. Continue cooking until meat is very tender and most of liquid is absorbed. (The meat mixture can be cooled and refrigerated for 1-2 days at this point, or frozen.) Add ground almonds and simmer for 10 minutes. Add cream and cilantro at the last minute before serving and heat just to serving temperature. Serve with rice.

*To clarify butter, melt 1 cube of butter in a small saucepan over low heat. When butter foams, skim off foam with a tablespoon. Carefully pour off clear liquid and leave milky solids in bottom of pan. Use clear butter liquid; discard milky solids.

Beachboy's Barbecued Leg of Lamb

Serves 6

If you're not into boning, ask your butcher to butterfly a leg of lamb for you. It will cook evenly and be a dream to carve.

1 (6-7 lb.) leg of lamb, boned and butterflied
1 medium onion, thinly sliced

Marinade:
2 cloves garlic, crushed
¾ cup olive oil
¼ cup red wine vinegar
1 tbs. whole grain mustard **or** Dijon mustard
1 tsp. salt
1 tsp. dried oregano
1 tsp. dried basil
freshly ground pepper

Carefully trim all fat off leg of lamb. Place a large plastic bag in a flat pan. Place lamb in bag with onions. Mix marinade ingredients together and pour over lamb. Close bag with tie and refrigerate overnight, turning once or twice to distribute marinade evenly. Remove lamb from refrigerator 1-2 hours before you plan to barbecue. Remove from marinade, scraping off most of onions and barbecue over a hot fire about 15 minutes each side for medium rare meat. Remove to a cutting board and carve into thin slices.

Marinated Lamb Chops

Serves 6

John experimented many times in developing this recipe. He's been serving his specialty to his wife and daughters and to delighted guests for years.

1 cup red wine **or** rosé wine
juice of two lemons
2 tsp. oregano, dried **or** 4 tsp. fresh, finely chopped
2 tsp. mint, fresh **or** dried
4 cloves garlic, finely minced
salt and freshly ground pepper
6 lamb chops, well trimmed

In a shallow glass baking dish, combine wine, lemon juice, oregano, mint, garlic, salt and pepper. Add lamb chops, cover with plastic wrap and refrigerate 8-24 hours. Turn chops often. Remove from refrigerator and return to room temperature before cooking. Grill on a barbecue or broil in oven about 5 minutes per side. Meanwhile, heat remaining marinade to a light boil, reduce heat and simmer 10 minutes. Serve in a bowl to pour over chops and rice, potatoes or noodles.

Lamb Stew

All the lovely flavors "marry" and make a really delicious dish.

2 lbs. lamb, cut into 1½" cubes
2 tbs. olive oil **or** vegetable oil
1 large onion, sliced
3-4 carrots, cut into ½" slices
4 stalks celery, sliced
2 medium tomatoes, peeled, seeded, chopped
½ tsp. dill weed
½ cup beef broth
1 bay leaf
salt and freshly ground pepper
1 cup raw peas
3-4 tbs. parsley, chopped

In a skillet, brown lamb cubes in oil. Remove from skillet and set aside. Add onion, carrots and celery to skillet and sauté 4-5 minutes, scraping up brown bits from bottom of pan. Place meat in a casserole and top with sautéed vegetables, tomatoes, dill weed, beef broth, bay leaf, salt and pepper. Cover and simmer about 1 hour. Add peas and cook an additional 10 minutes. Remove bay leaf. Sprinkle with parsley and serve with rice or mashed potatoes.

Lamb and Vegetable Kebobs

Serves 6

The American Lamb Council developed this light, delicious, fool-proof recipe. Lamb lovers line up!

1½ lbs. lamb, cut into 1¼" cubes
½ cup olive oil
¼ cup fresh lemon juice **or** lime juice
1 tsp. salt
½ tsp. paprika
½ tsp. onion powder
1 bay leaf, crumbled
½ tsp. dried thyme
¼ tsp. garlic powder
12 fresh mushrooms
12 small onions, boiled to tender crisp
12 strips (½" each) bell pepper

Arrange lamb cubes in a shallow glass baking dish. In a small bowl, thoroughly blend oil, lemon juice, salt, paprika, onion powder, bay leaf, thyme and garlic powder. Pour over lamb. Cover and refrigerate 6-8 hours, turning occasionally. Alternately thread lamb, mushrooms, onions and bell pepper on 6 skewers. Broil 3"-4" from source of heat (broiler or outdoor grill) for 13-16 minutes, brushing frequently with marinade and turning to brown evenly. Serve with rice pilaf.

Lamb Curry

Jesse says this is a snap if you have some left-over roast lamb. For your next party, fill a large mixing bowl with ice and a variety of beers and use it for a centerpiece. This spicy curry is great with beer.

4 tbs. butter
5 tbs. curry powder
2 large onions, thinly sliced
1 large clove garlic, minced
2 large stalks celery, chopped
½ green pepper, chopped
1 large tart apple, unpeeled, chopped
2 carrots, thinly sliced
2 fresh tomatoes, coarsely chopped
½ tsp. salt

¼ tsp. thyme
2 bay leaves
1 (14 ozs.) can beef broth
2 cups water
4 tsp. cornstarch
3-4 cups cooked lamb, diced
3 cups uncooked rice, cooked
grated unsweetened coconut,
    chopped peanuts, chutney

Melt butter in a saucepan. Add curry powder and cook 2 minutes. Add onions, garlic, celery, green pepper, apple and carrots. Sauté 3-4 minutes and add tomatoes, salt, spices, broth and water. Simmer uncovered about 2 hours. Strain through a large sieve, pressing as much vegetable pulp through sieve as possible. Return sieved mixture to pan. Dissolve cornstarch in 2 tbs. water and add to sauce. Cook, stirring until sauce thickens. Add lamb and cook a few minutes to blend flavors. Serve over rice. Pass grated unsweetened coconut, chopped peanuts and chutney. A fresh fruit salad with pineapple or melon chunks makes a nice cooling accompaniment.

Roy's Baked Lamb and Rice Casserole

Serves 4-6

Roy serves this hearty dish with garlic bread, a tossed green salad and a bottle of good red wine. He gets a lot of compliments.

2 lbs. lean, boneless lamb
2 tbs. oil
2 tbs. butter
1 medium onion, chopped
1 small red pepper, diced
¼ tsp. red pepper flakes
1½ cups uncooked long grain rice
1 tsp. salt
½ tsp. dried sweet basil
½ tsp. dried oregano
1 (8 ozs.) can tomato sauce
2 (10 ozs. each) cans beef broth
⅓ cup dry sherry **or** red wine

Preheat oven to 350°. Trim lamb of all fat and cut into 1"-1½" cubes. Heat oil in a large heavy skillet and brown lamb cubes. Remove meat and pour off all fat. Add butter, onions, red pepper and red pepper flakes. Cook slowly until onion and peppers are soft but not brown. Add rice, salt, basil and oregano. Cook 3-4 minutes until rice is opaque. Add lamb, tomato sauce, beef broth and sherry. Bring to a boil, simmer 4-5 minutes and pour into a casserole with a tightly fitting lid. Bake at 350° for 45 minutes or until liquid is absorbed and rice is tender.

Chicken

You guessed it. The favored chicken is ... fried chicken! But men like chicken prepared in many other ways: dressed up in delicious sauces and stir-fried are two other favorites. Here are those and more.

On page 75, Michael Surfburger (page 55) ▶

On page 76, Daryl Jim's Western Barbecue (page 52) ▶

Baked Garlic Chicken

Serves 4

For men who say they prefer a baked version of chicken, this recipe is a fantastic blend of garlic and herbs. The drippings make wonderful gravy to pour over mashed potatoes or biscuits. A tossed green salad and corn on the cob make this a man's meal.

8 pieces chicken (breasts, thighs, drumsticks)
½ tsp. oregano
½ tsp. paprika
salt and freshly ground pepper
¼ cup polyunsaturated margarine

5 large cloves garlic, finely minced
1 tsp. dried basil
1 tbs. fresh **or** dried parsley
1 tbs. sherry **or** white wine
2 tbs. olive oil

Season chicken pieces with oregano, paprika, salt and pepper. Place in a 9" x 13" baking dish and cover with slices of margarine. Bake at 375° for 45-60 minutes or until chicken is browned. Meanwhile, mix garlic, basil, parsley, sherry and olive oil until well blended. Spread over chicken pieces. Return to oven and bake 15-20 minutes more or until chicken is tender.

Juan's Orange Chicken

Serves 6

This simple recipe is a fantastic tasting chicken dish. Invite some friends for brunch.

6 chicken breast halves, skinned
1 (6 ozs.) can frozen orange juice concentrate, thawed
1 (1.5 ozs.) pkg. dry onion soup mix
1 orange, sliced

In a 9" x 13" dish, prepared with nonstick vegetable spray, arrange chicken breasts. In a small bowl, mix dry onion soup mix with orange juice concentrate. Pour over chicken, making sure that each piece is well coated. Bake at 375° for 30-40 minutes. During last 5 minutes, place a slice of orange on each piece of chicken.

◄ On page 77, Jamie
Fried Chicken (page 80) and Spicy Noodle Salad (page 31)

◄ On page 78, Rod
Classic Shrimp Cocktail Sauce (page 9)

Fried Chicken

This is the #1 chicken choice of men.

3 lbs. chicken pieces
¾ cup flour
1 tsp. salt
½ tsp. pepper
2 tsp. paprika

½ tsp. dried thyme
½ tsp. poultry seasoning
½-1 cup milk
⅓-½ cup vegetable oil (about ¼" in bottom of skillet)

In a paper bag, mix flour, salt, pepper, paprika, thyme and poultry seasoning. Dip chicken (a few pieces at a time) into milk, shaking to remove excess, and then shake pieces in bag until well coated with flour and seasonings. Pour oil into a skillet over medium high heat. Arrange chicken in a single layer without crowding. Brown slowly for about 15 minutes. When pink juices start to show on top, turn and brown the other side for 15 minutes. After all pieces are browned, add 3-4 tbs. water and cover. Cook 10-12 minutes more. Remove cover and cook chicken 2 minutes per side to crisp.

Pepper Chicken

These spicy chicken pieces are great barbecued over a hot fire. Serve them with **Crisp Oven Wedges**, *page 112, and a big green salad.*

¼ cup lime **or** lemon juice
2 tsp. freshly ground black pepper
1 tsp. red hot pepper flakes, crushed
½ tsp. cumin

3 tbs. olive oil
salt
8 chicken thighs **or** other chicken pieces

Combine lime juice, pepper, pepper flakes, cumin, olive oil and salt. Place chicken thighs in a bowl and cover with lime juice mixture, marinating about 2 hours, or overnight. Remove from marinade and grill over a very hot fire for about 10 minutes a side, or until juices run clear.

Breast of Chicken in Champagne

Serves 4-6

Patrick enjoys preparing this rich and elegant dish and suggests that it is a good company dinner. Rice pilaf and glazed carrots are the perfect accompaniment.

6-8 boneless chicken breast halves
1 tbs. flour
½ tsp. salt
½ tsp. white pepper
6 tbs. butter

¾ lb. fresh mushrooms, sliced
1 cup whipping cream
1 tbs. sweet basil
⅓ cup champagne

Pound breasts between waxed paper sheets until flat. Combine flour, salt and pepper; dust breasts with mixture. In a medium skillet, sauté mushrooms in 4 tbs. butter. Remove and set aside. Add 2 tbs. butter to the skillet and brown the chicken pieces 3-4 minutes per side. Cover breasts with cooked sliced mushrooms. Cover and cook over low heat for 10 minutes. Add cream and sweet basil and simmer 10 minutes more. Remove breasts to a warm platter. Add champagne to pan and cook over high heat until sauce is thickened, stirring often to avoid sticking. Pour sauce over chicken breasts.

Baked Mustard Chicken

Serves 4

Frank's mustard chicken is great to pack up and take to the beach or on a bike ride. You can expand the recipe for any number of people.

2 whole chicken breasts, **or** 4 large legs
4-6 tsp. Dijon mustard

Preheat oven to 375°. Carefully slip your fingers under skin of chicken breasts or drumsticks and loosen it. Put about 1 tsp. Dijon mustard under the skin of each piece. Paint the top of the skin with a light coating of mustard. Place on a baking rack in a foil-lined pan and bake for about 50 minutes. Delicious hot or cold. Refrigerate if you don't serve immediately.

Modenda Chicken

Michael says this recipe is good for quick preparation of a special meal. He says, "Don't tell guests that it is also good for them because it's low in calories and cholesterol."

l lb. mushrooms
4 chicken breast halves
2 tbs. flour
⅛ tsp. freshly ground pepper
¼ tsp. thyme

1 tbs. oil
8 cloves garlic, peeled
1 cup chicken broth
¼ cup balsamic vinegar
2 bay leaves

Clean mushrooms; cut ½ lb. into quarters, ½ lb. into slices. In a shallow bowl, mix flour, pepper and thyme. Heat oil in a large heavy skillet. Coat chicken with flour mixture and cook in oil 3 minutes on one side. Add garlic. Turn chicken and add mushrooms; cook 3 minutes more and add broth. When sizzling stops, add vinegar and bay leaves. Cover and cook over medium heat 10 minutes. Remove chicken to a serving platter. Discard garlic and bay leaves. Reduce sauce until thickened. Pour over chicken and serve.

Mediterranean Chicken

This recipe gives a delightfully different flavor to chicken.

¼ cup olive oil
3 chicken breasts, halved, skinned
½ tsp. thyme
1 medium white onion, sliced
1 large lemon, thinly sliced
½ cup large green olives, pitted, whole

In a heavy skillet, brown chicken pieces in olive oil over medium high heat. Sprinkle with thyme. Arrange slices of onion and lemon over chicken pieces; add whole olives. Reduce heat, cover and cook for 45-60 minutes or until chicken is tender. Nice served with rice pilaf.

Chicken Marengo

Serves 4-5

Simple but good, here is Chuck's favorite chicken recipe for the tennis crowd.

2 tbs. butter **or** margarine
1 tbs. olive oil
8-10 pieces of chicken, skin removed
1 large onion, chopped
1 clove garlic, minced
½ cup dry white wine

2 tbs. tomato paste
1 tbs. water
½ lb. fresh mushrooms, sliced
salt and freshly ground pepper
minced parsley

In a large skillet, heat butter and olive oil; brown chicken. Add onion, garlic and wine; simmer 5 minutes. In a small bowl, mix tomato paste and water. Spread over chicken pieces. Cover pan and simmer gently for 30 minutes or until chicken is tender. Add sliced mushrooms and cook 10 minutes more. Sprinkle with minced parsley. Serve over rice.

Honey Glazed Chicken

Serves 4-6

Marinate this chicken the night before and bake it while you relax before dinner. This is good hot or at room temperature.

6 whole chicken legs, skin removed
½ cup soy sauce
⅓ cup honey

2 tbs. vegetable oil
1 clove garlic, minced
1 tsp. fresh ginger, grated

Combine soy sauce, honey, oil, garlic and ginger and pour over chicken legs. Marinate in a food storage bag placed in a bowl. Refrigerate for several hours or overnight, turning bag occasionally so all pieces are covered by marinade. Preheat oven to 375°. Line shallow baking pan with foil. Remove chicken pieces from marinade, place on foil and discard marinade. Bake for 25 minutes. Turn chicken pieces over, increase oven heat to 400° and bake for about 20-25 minutes longer. Remove to a plate and cool slightly before serving.

Chicken Livers in Wine Sauce

Serves 4

This recipe is from Mike, a man who really loves to cook. He says this recipe is so good, even his lovely wife, who doesn't like chicken livers, will eat them with him.

⅓ cup water
⅓ cup dry red wine
1 tbs. cornstarch
4 slices bacon, cut into ½" slices

5 green onions, thinly sliced
1 lb. chicken livers
¼ lb. mushrooms, sliced

In a small bowl, mix water, wine and cornstarch and set aside. In a skillet, cook bacon until crisp. Remove bacon and set aside. Cook green onions and mushrooms in bacon fat for 2-3 minutes; remove and set aside. Stir-fry chicken livers in the same skillet for 7-8 minutes or until no longer pink. Add liquid-cornstarch mixture, bacon, green onions and mushrooms. Stir to coat livers with sauce and allow to thicken. Cook just until hot and thickened. Serve over cooked rice.

Dale's Turkey Loaf

Serves 10-12

Dale uses turkey to make a different style meat loaf for the gang. Makes great sandwiches, too. He says it is best if made a day before eating.

2 lbs. ground turkey
2 large carrots, peeled, grated
2 medium potatoes, peeled, grated
1 large onion, grated
1 (4 ozs.) can black olives, chopped

4 ozs. saltine crackers, crushed
6 eggs
1 (18 ozs.) bottle barbecue sauce
1 cup catsup

Mix turkey with all ingredients except catsup. Place in a 13" x 9" x 2" baking pan. Bake at 350° for 1 hour and 15 minutes. Glaze top with catsup and return to oven for 5 minutes.

Chicken Oriental Stir-Fry

Each serving of this delicious chicken dish has only 140 calories and 4 grams of fat.

1 tbs. oil
2 chicken breasts, skin and bone removed, cut into ½" strips
2 slices fresh ginger root, minced
1 clove garlic, minced
2 tsp. vegetable oil
1 lb. fresh vegetables, chopped (carrots, green onions, celery, mushrooms, snow peas)

Sauce:
1 heaping tbs. cornstarch
3 tbs. rice vinegar
½ cup chicken broth
2 tsp. soy sauce
¼ tsp. hot chili oil (optional)

Heat 1 tbs. oil in a skillet or wok. Sauté garlic and ginger. Add chicken and stir-fry until lightly browned (approximately 2-3 minutes). Remove from pan and set aside. Heat 1 tsp. oil in the same skillet or wok, add hard, crunchy vegetables (carrots, celery) and stir-fry 2-3 minutes. Add tender vegetables (green onions, mushrooms, snow peas) and stir-fry 1-2 minutes longer. Return chicken to pan. Combine sauce ingredients and pour over vegetable-chicken mixture. Heat and stir continuously until thickened. Serve over steamed rice.

Variation: Choose some hard and tender vegetables for each stir-fry.

Hard		Tender	
Carrots	Cauliflower	Green onions	Spinach
Celery	Water chestnuts	Snow peas	Bok choy
White onion	Asparagas	Bean sprouts	Mushrooms
Jicama	Bell pepper		
Broccoli	Bamboo shoots		

Cashew Chicken

Here is a delicious and heart-healthy stir-fry. Arrange the ingredients beautifully on a tray and cook it at the table in an electric fry pan or wok.

2 chicken breasts, skinned, boned
½ lb. pea pods **or** broccoli flowerettes
½ lb. mushrooms, washed, sliced
4 green onions
1 (8 ozs.) can bamboo shoots, drained, rinsed
1 cup chicken broth
1 tbs. soy sauce
2 tbs. cornstarch
½ tsp. sugar
1 tsp. oil
¼ cup cashew nuts, dry roasted

Cut chicken breasts into 1" cubes. Arrange on a tray. Remove ends and strings from pea pods or chop broccoli. Add to tray with sliced mushrooms. Cut green part of onions into 1" lengths; slash both ends lengthwise several times, making small fans. Slice white part of onions into ¼" slices. Slice bamboo shoots. Pour chicken broth into a small pitcher. Mix soy sauce, cornstarch and sugar together and add to pitcher. Place oil and nuts in small containers. Arrange at the table with an electric fry pan or wok. Add oil to pan; add chicken and cook quickly, stirring until it turns opaque. Add peas and mushrooms; pour in broth, cover and simmer 2 minutes. Add bamboo shoots. Stir soy sauce mixture into pan juices and cook until sauce is thickened, stirring constantly. Simmer 2 more minutes. Mix in green onion, sprinkle with nuts and serve on hot rice.

Chicken Gumbo

Serves 6

Another man-pleasing chicken recipe, this one includes sausage. Serve it over rice with garlic bread and a crisp salad.

3 slices bacon, cut into ½" pieces
12 chicken thighs, skin removed
flour for dredging thighs
1 celery stalk, diced
2 onions, chopped
1 green pepper, chopped
1 (14 ozs.) can tomato pieces with juice
½ tsp. thyme
¼ tsp. white pepper
6-8 drops Tabasco
3 cups chicken stock
½ cup white wine
1 (10 ozs.) pkg. frozen sliced okra, thawed
2 hot Italian sausages, cooked
½ cup ham, diced (optional)
salt and freshly ground pepper
6-7 cups cooked rice

Fry bacon in a large skillet. Remove bacon, reserving fat. Dredge chicken in flour and brown in bacon fat, adding oil if necessary. Remove chicken; add onion, green pepper and celery and sauté until soft. Add tomatoes with their juice, thyme, pepper, Tabasco, chicken stock and wine to skillet. Bring to a boil and add bacon, chicken, okra, sausage and ham. Simmer, covered, 30 minutes, stirring occasionally. Remove chicken and pull meat from bones in fairly large pieces. Return to gumbo and cook, uncovered, 20 minutes. Add salt and pepper to taste. Place rice in bowls and ladle gumbo over rice.

Jim's Chicken Supreme

Jim says he uses this as a peace offering and it has returned him to good grace several times. If you really want to make an impression, garnish the chicken breasts with fresh chanterelle mushrooms or crab legs.

2 tbs. butter
½ small onion, diced
¼ tsp. thyme
¼ tsp. sweet basil
salt and freshly ground pepper
1 cup fresh bread crumbs
¼ cup Madeira **or** sherry
½ (10 ozs.) can mushroom soup
4 boneless chicken breasts, skin removed, pounded flat
¼ lb. ham, thinly sliced
¼ lb. mild cheese, thinly sliced
fresh chanterelle mushroom slices, sautéed, or
   fresh cooked crab legs for garnish

Melt butter and cook onion until soft. Add thyme, basil, salt, pepper and bread crumbs and mix well. Whisk wine and soup together and pour about ½ sauce into a baking dish. Place 2 chicken breasts in dish, top each with 1 slice of ham, ½ bread crumb mixture, another slice of ham, 1-2 slices of cheese and the remaining chicken breast. Coat the top with remaining sauce. Bake 30 minutes uncovered at 400°. Remove from oven and add garnish; bake another 5-7 minutes to heat through. Allow dish to cool a few minutes before serving so layers will set up.

Cornish Game Hens with Cabbage

Serves 4

Duane's recipe makes a special company dinner. Serve it with oven browned potatoes or rice pilaf, and a good pinot noir wine.

4 Cornish game hens
2 small heads green cabbage
1 tbs. butter
1 tbs. vegetable oil
4 cloves garlic, minced
⅓ cup pine nuts
½ tsp. nutmeg
salt and freshly ground pepper

Cut game hens down the back, trim excess skin and open. Press birds, bone side down, so they are somewhat flattened. Season with salt, pepper and ¼ tsp. nutmeg. Cut cabbage into 1" squares, separate leaves and sauté in hot butter and oil with garlic and pine nuts until cabbage begins to turn opaque, about 8-10 minutes. Season lightly with salt, pepper and remaining nutmeg. Transfer cabbage to a baking dish and place game hens, bone side down, on top of cabbage. Bake at 350° for 1 hour. Drain off juices and pour over game hens just before serving.

Seafood

We ran into a few men who didn't like fish, but most men appear to be seafood enthusiasts, and they like all kinds of fish. Although salmon and sautéed shrimp were mentioned most often, men listed almost every kind of fish you can think of. Very few asked for fried fish; broiled, baked and steamed were favorite ways of preparation.

Brian ▶
Broiled Salmon (page 98)

Baked Snapper with Seafood Cream Sauce   Serves 2

Dinner for two: add rice pilaf, a fresh veggie salad, candlelight, soft music and the love of your life.

12-16 ozs. fish fillets
salt and freshly ground pepper
2 tbs. olive oil
2-3 ozs. salad shrimp

1 clove garlic, minced
1 tbs. shallots, minced
4 ozs. white wine
6 ozs. heavy cream

Arrange fish in a greased baking pan, season with salt and pepper, cover and bake at 375° for 15 minutes, until fish is opaque. While fish is baking, make sauce: in a medium skillet over high heat, sauté shrimp, garlic and shallots in 2 tbs. olive oil. Add wine and juice from baked fish. Reduce liquid to ½ volume over high heat. Reduce heat, add heavy cream and simmer 1-2 minutes. Pour over fish and serve.

Oven Fried Fish   Serves 2

This fish recipe is a good one when you want something delicious in a hurry.

1 lb. fish fillets
½ cup milk
½ cup fine Italian bread crumbs
½ tsp. oregano
dash hot pepper flakes
salt and freshly ground pepper
2 tbs. melted butter

Dip fish in milk and roll in bread crumbs. Place in a greased baking pan. Season with oregano, hot pepper flakes, salt and pepper. Drizzle with melted butter. Bake at 450° for 10-12 minutes, or until fish flakes easily with a fork.

Variation: Arrange slices of fresh lemon on the bottom of the baking pan before placing fish in pan, and place fresh tomato slices on top of fish.

◄ **Steve**
Vegetables and Soups (pages 129-141)

Stuffed Clam Shells

David says this can be a main course or will serve 8 people as a fantastic appetizer.

2 (6½ ozs. each) cans chopped clams with liquid **or** 1 can chopped clams plus
   1 lb. fresh steamer clams, steamed, shelled, chopped
juice of ½ lemon
1 cup fresh French bread crumbs
½ cup Parmesan cheese, grated
1 clove garlic, minced
2 tbs. fresh parsley, finely chopped
½ cup butter, melted
salt and freshly ground pepper
12-16 empty, cleaned clam shells **or** individual au gratin dishes

In a medium bowl, mix clams with liquid, lemon juice, bread crumbs, Parmesan cheese, garlic, fresh parsley, melted butter, salt and pepper. Spoon into clam shells or dishes. Do not overly fill shells. Place filled shells on a baking sheet and bake at 350° for 15 minutes or until stuffing is bubbly. Then broil until tops are golden, about 2 minutes, watching carefully to avoid burning.

Seafood Stew

Serves 8-10

Milford sent us this recipe. When he serves it, everyone has second helpings. His regular guests have nicknamed him Chowder Milf.

1 lb. **each** chopped clams, crab meat, baby shrimp,
  small scallops and petite oysters
1 (16 ozs.) can clam juice
1 qt. half-and-half
2 qts. milk
¼ tsp. ground bay leaf
½ tsp. ground white pepper
½ tsp. thyme
½ tsp. basil
⅛ tsp. cayenne pepper
¼ tsp. oregano
1 tsp. curry powder
½ cup butter
salt and freshly ground pepper

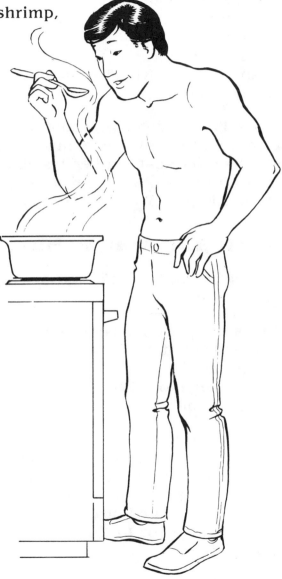

In a 6-quart Dutch oven, cook seafood in clam juice over low heat for about 15 minutes. Stir occasionally to avoid scorching. Increase heat slightly and slowly add half-and-half and milk, stirring constantly until hot. More milk may be added for a thinner stew. Add seasonings and butter and cover. Simmer about 30 minutes. Add additional seasoning and salt to taste, cover and simmer about 15 minutes more. Stew should be very thick with seafood as you serve it. Serve with oyster crackers, French bread and white wine.

Oyster Wine Stew

Serves 2

Eat this in front of a glowing fire with crusty garlic bread and your true love. That's what George, who sent this recipe, recommends.

1 cup onion, chopped
2 tbs. fresh parsley, chopped
2 tbs. butter
1 tbs. soy sauce
1 tsp. crushed dried thyme
½ bay leaf

dash Tabasco sauce
1 pt. fresh oysters
2 cups light cream
1 cup cheddar cheese, shredded
½ cup white wine

In a large saucepan, sauté onion and parsley in butter until tender but not brown. Stir in soy sauce, thyme, bay leaf and Tabasco. Add oysters. Cook and stir over low heat until edges of oysters begin to curl, about 3 minutes. Stir in milk and cream and heat through, being careful not to boil. Add cheese and stir until melted. Remove from heat; discard bay leaf. Add wine and serve.

Herb and Garlic Shrimp Kebobs

Serves 4

John loves to cook, and shrimp is one of his favorites, just as it is with many men.

1 lb. shrimp, peeled, deveined
  (26-30 count per lb.)
¼ tsp. salt
½ tsp. oregano
½ tsp. thyme

½ cup butter
4 cloves garlic, finely minced
1 tbs. parsley, minced
16 whole fresh mushrooms
16 cherry tomatoes

In a medium bowl, toss shrimp with salt, oregano and thyme. Chill for 30 minutes. In a medium skillet, melt butter and sauté minced garlic and parsley; set aside. Thread 3 shrimp on each of 8 skewers, spacing with cherry tomatoes and mushrooms. Place on a lightly greased baking pan. Brush each kebob with garlic butter, being especially generous on the mushrooms. Bake in a 350° oven for 12-15 minutes, being careful not to overcook. Serve on a bed of rice pilaf.

Spinach Stuffed Poached Trout

This is another recipe from popular chef Horst Mager.

2 boneless trout (8 ozs. each)
1 tbs. olive oil
1 tbs. onion, chopped
2 cloves garlic, minced
1 lb. spinach leaves, thoroughly washed
juice of 1 lemon
salt and freshly ground pepper
1 tbs. white wine
2 tbs. water

In a medium skillet, heat olive oil. Sauté chopped onion and minced garlic. Add spinach leaves and sauté until leaves are just wilted. Fill trout cavities with spinach mixture. Place trout in a microwave dish and sprinkle with lemon juice, salt and pepper. Drizzle white wine and water over fish. Cover with plastic wrap and cook in a microwave oven on high power for 3 minutes.

Sauce:
1 tbs. olive oil
4 large fresh tomatoes, peeled, seeded, diced
1 clove garlic, minced
1 tbs. onion, chopped
1 tsp. dried basil **or** 2 leaves of fresh, chopped
pinch sugar
1 tbs. white wine
salt and freshly ground pepper

Sauté tomato in olive oil. Add garlic, onion, basil, sugar, white wine, salt and pepper. Simmer for 5 minutes. To serve: carefully remove skin from both sides of trout. Place tomato sauce on a platter and arrange trout on top. Serve with plain boiled potatoes.

Barbecued Salmon

Serves 4

Salmon was a favorite from one side of the country to the other. This recipe is from Jim, in Oregon.

4 salmon fillets, 6-7 ozs. each, **or**
   4 salmon steaks, 8 ozs. each
¼ cup butter
2 cloves garlic, minced
1 tbs. shallots, minced

1 tbs. scallions, minced
1 tbs. fresh tarragon
1 tbs. fresh basil
salt and freshly ground pepper
2 tbs. parsley, chopped

Place salmon on a large piece of heavy foil, turning up the edges to make a shallow dish. Melt butter in a saucepan; sauté garlic, shallots and scallions. Add fresh tarragon, basil, salt, pepper and parsley. Pour this mixture over fish. Start briquettes with cedar chips and heat charcoal. Place salmon with foil on barbecue grill and cover. Cook 15-20 minutes until fish flakes easily with a fork. Serve immediately.

Broiled Salmon

Serves 4

This version of the #1 favorite was sent to us by Ed, in Maryland.

¼ cup butter
¼ cup olive oil
2 tbs. lemon juice
1 tsp. lemon peel, grated
1 tsp. seasoning salt
1 tsp. tarragon

¾ tsp. garlic powder
½ tsp. marjoram
⅛ tsp. red pepper
freshly ground black pepper
2 salmon steaks, 1 lb. each

Melt butter and combine with olive oil, lemon juice and remaining ingredients. Brush salmon with ½ of mixture. Broil 7 minutes. Turn and brush salmon with remaining mixture; broil another 7 minutes or until salmon flakes easily with a fork.

Baked Salmon

Ken prepares this delicately sweet flavored salmon, a little different and delicious.

1 salmon (3-4 lbs.), filleted, skin removed
½ cup butter
¼-½ cup brown sugar

1 lemon, thinly sliced
juice of 1 lemon
1 medium onion, diced

Place each salmon fillet on lightly buttered aluminum foil. Spread each with butter and cover each with ½ the brown sugar, lemon slices, diced onion and lemon juice. Fold foil to form a packet, leaving a small opening for steam. Place packets on a cookie sheet and bake at 375° for 15-20 minutes or until fish flakes. Serve with steamed broccoli.

Larry's Deviled Crab

Deviled crab makes a good first course or lunch dish with a crisp green salad and a bottle of good white wine.

1 lb. crab meat, picked over to remove shells
2 tbs. butter
4 green onions, minced
1 medium stalk celery, finely chopped
2 tbs. red bell pepper, finely chopped

¼ cup cracker crumbs
3-4 drops Tabasco
2 tbs. heavy cream
2 tbs. parsley, chopped
1 tbs. butter

Melt butter in a small skillet and sauté green onions, celery and red pepper 3-4 minutes until slightly softened. In a medium mixing bowl, combine crab, crushed cracker crumbs, Tabasco, cooked onion mixture, heavy cream and parsley. Mix well, adding a little more cream if crab seems dry. Place in buttered individual au gratin dishes or an 8"-9" pie plate. Dot with butter and bake at 375° for about 20 minutes or until heated through. Run under the broiler to brown lightly.

Halibut with Dijon Mustard Sauce

Serves 4

Chef Brett Meisner of the Sea Hag Restaurant contributes another great recipe. He recommends his specialty sauce for just about any fish.

4 halibut steaks (8 ozs. each)
4 tsp. butter
salt and freshly ground pepper
1 small onion, sliced
1 lemon, thinly sliced
½ cup white wine

Sauce:
2 tsp. butter
½ cup whipping cream
1 tbs. Dijon mustard
dash white pepper
dash salt

chopped parsley
lemon slices

Place fish in a lightly greased shallow casserole dish. Dot with butter and sprinkle with salt and pepper. Top each steak with sliced lemon and onion. Pour wine over fish and bake at 400° for 10 minutes or until fish flakes easily with a fork. To make sauce: in a small skillet, melt butter, pour in whipping cream and blend. Simmer until sauce is reduced by half. Stir in mustard, pepper and salt. Pour over fish, sprinkle with chopped parsley and garnish with lemon slices.

Escabeche

This is another dish that is better the next day. Use a firm fleshed fish such as red snapper, halibut, orange roughy or sea bass. Makes a great summer supper with hot garlic bread and small boiled potatoes.

1 lb. fresh red snapper fillets
flour seasoned with salt and pepper
¼ cup peanut oil
2 tbs. full-flavored olive oil
1 medium onion, thinly sliced
1 small carrot, thinly sliced
3 cloves garlic, smashed
½ cup cider vinegar
¼ cup water
1 tbs. lemon juice
1 tsp. brown sugar
salt and freshly ground pepper
dash red pepper flakes
½ tsp. dried thyme **or** 2 sprigs fresh
1 tbs. white raisins
1 tsp. capers
black olives for garnish

Cut each fish fillet into 2-3 medium pieces. Dredge in seasoned flour. Heat peanut oil in a large skillet and quickly sauté fish 3-4 minutes each side until fish flakes. Remove and place in a deep-sided pan or dish. Discard oil, wipe out pan, add olive oil to pan and heat over medium heat. Add sliced onion, carrots and garlic cloves. Cook 2-3 minutes until onion and carrot soften. Add vinegar, water, lemon juice, brown sugar, salt, pepper, red pepper flakes, thyme and raisins to skillet. Bring to a boil. Pour over fish, add capers, cool to room temperature, and then cover and refrigerate. Serve at room temperature.

Variation: Add red pepper strips and pine nuts in place of carrots and raisins.

Basque Style Rice and Clams

Here is Ray's easy recipe for a delicious casserole. Serve it with a crisp salad for a pre-ski get-together, or fill individual au gratin dishes for a first course with a good chardonnay.

3 (6½ ozs. each) cans chopped clams
1 (8 ozs.) bottle clam juice
⅓ cup olive oil
½ cup onion, minced
¼ tsp. hot pepper flakes
1½ cups uncooked long grain rice
2 large garlic cloves, minced
½ cup parsley, finely chopped
1 large tomato, peeled, seeded, chopped
pinch of saffron threads (optional)
1 tsp. salt
freshly ground pepper

Drain clams, reserving juice. Combine reserved juice with bottled clam juice plus enough water to make 3¼ cups total liquid. Heat olive oil in a large heavy skillet. Sauté onion 5-6 minutes until soft. Add rice, stir until well coated with oil, and add remaining ingredients. Bring to a rapid boil, cover tightly and reduce heat to barest simmer. Cook for 20 minutes without lifting lid. Stir in clams. Check rice to see if it is cooked and add ¼ cup additional water if rice is not done. Cook covered for a few more minutes.

Lynn's Seafood Sauté with Rice

This outstanding dish takes only 20 minutes preparation time. Lynn, who loves to cook, says frozen shellfish can be substituted, but it won't be quite the same. Include chardonnay or chenin blanc wine and drink the rest with your dinner.

4-6 ozs. fresh shrimp
4-6 ozs. fresh scallops
4-6 ozs. fresh crab meat
2 tbs. clarified butter
2 cloves garlic, minced
3 green onions, chopped
½ green bell pepper, diced
½ red bell pepper, diced
4 medium mushrooms, sliced
⅓ cup chardonnay or chenin blanc wine
1 tbs. flour
cooked rice
lemon wedges and parsley sprigs for garnish

In a 12" skillet over medium heat, melt butter and sauté garlic, green onion, green and red peppers and mushrooms. When vegetables are still crisp tender, add shrimp, scallops and crab. Add wine and sauté until scallops are opaque. Sprinkle with flour and stir gently until thickened. Serve over rice. Garnish with lemon wedges and parsley.

Tip: Serve with fresh Brussels sprouts or broccoli served in orange shells.

Sautéed Shrimp

Les entered this in our Men's Cooking Contest. It's an excellent version of sautéed shrimp.

½ cup butter
1 medium onion, chopped
2 cloves garlic, minced
½ cup brandy
1 tsp. chicken bouillon crystals
1 tbs. brown sugar
1½ lbs. large shrimp, peeled, deveined

1 tbs. sherry
1 tbs. lemon juice
1 medium tomato, peeled, seeded, chopped
salt and freshly ground pepper
cooked white rice
parsley, chopped, for garnish

In a deep skillet, melt butter and add onion, garlic, brandy, bouillon crystals, brown sugar and shrimp. Simmer until shrimp are almost cooked, about 2 minutes. Add sherry, lemon juice, tomato, salt and pepper. Simmer 1-2 minutes more. Serve over a bed of white rice and sprinkle with fresh parsley.

Fried Calamari

Everyone likes crisp fried calamari! Here is a simple but terrific recipe.

2 lbs. squid, cleaned, cut into 3/8" rings
2 cups flour
salt and freshly ground pepper
¼ tsp. cayenne
oil for deep frying (about 3 cups)

Dry squid with paper towels. Heat oil to 375°. Place flour, salt, pepper and cayenne in a small paper sack, add about ⅓ of the squid and shake to coat with flour. Place floured squid in a large sieve and shake to remove excess flour. Deep fry 3-4 minutes until crisp and lightly browned. Repeat with remaining squid, after allowing oil to come up to temperature again. Serve with seafood cocktail sauce or tartar sauce.

Steve ▶
Sweet Breakfast Treats (page 143)

Shrimp Chow Mein

Serves 2-3

Cook this dish with your S.O. (significant other) to make quick work of peeling the shrimp and preparing the vegetables.

6 ozs. thin, fresh Chinese style noodles **or** 4 ozs. dried spaghetti
2 tsp. cornstarch
1 tbs. **plus** 1 tsp. soy sauce
1 egg white
¼ tsp. white pepper
6 ozs. small raw shrimp, peeled, deveined, cut in half lengthwise
6 tbs. vegetable oil
1 large clove garlic, peeled, smashed
¼" slice fresh ginger
3 green onions, thinly sliced
6 ozs. small mushrooms, thinly sliced
6 ozs. fresh bean sprouts **or** thinly sliced raw cabbage
1 tsp. sesame oil

Cook noodles and drain well. Combine cornstarch, 1 tsp. soy sauce, egg white and white pepper. Pour over shrimp, mix well and set aside. Add 2 tbs. vegetable oil to wok or large nonstick skillet and cook garlic and ginger over high heat until slightly brown. Remove garlic and ginger pieces and discard. Add cooked noodles to skillet, stir to coat with oil and allow to brown lightly on all sides. Turn out onto a plate covered with paper towels. Add 2 more tbs. oil to skillet; when hot, add shrimp mixture. Stir quickly for 1-2 minutes until shrimp are opaque and firm. Turn out on another plate covered with paper towels. Add remaining 2 tbs. oil to skillet and sauté onions and mushrooms for 1-2 minutes. Add bean sprouts and toss quickly. Return shrimp and cooked noodles to skillet and toss again. Remove from heat, add remaining tbs. of soy sauce and sesame oil, stir quickly and serve immediately on warm plates.

◄ Naim
Cheese Stix (page 146)

Mexican Fish Stew

Serves 3-4

Serve this hearty dish for a Sunday supper with a crisp salad. Sea bass, rock cod, halibut or salmon all are delicious fixed this way.

12 ozs. fresh pasta **or** 8 ozs. dried pasta (shells or bowties)
1 (28 ozs.) can tomato pieces with juice
1 large red pepper, peeled, seeded, chopped
2 tbs. olive oil
1 small onion, finely chopped
1 large clove garlic, finely chopped
1 tbs. anchovy paste
1 lb. sea bass, rock cod or other firm fleshed fish
1 tbs. lemon juice
salt and freshly ground pepper
1 tbs. olive oil
Parmesan cheese

Have pasta water hot and time pasta to be done when sauce is ready. Drain tomatoes, reserving juice. Heat olive oil in a heavy saucepan, sauté onion 3-4 minutes until soft but not brown. Add red pepper, garlic and anchovy paste and cook over low heat 2-3 minutes. Add tomato juice and reduce over high heat until about ½ of original volume. Cut fish into 1" pieces; add to saucepan with lemon juice and tomatoes. Simmer gently 2-3 minutes until fish is just done. Toss cooked, drained pasta with 1 tbs. olive oil and add sauce. Serve immediately on warm plates. Pass freshly grated Parmesan cheese.

Baked Scallops and Spinach

Serves 2

This great dish is just for the two of you. Frozen pouches of creamed spinach work well for this recipe.

1 (9 ozs.) pkg. frozen creamed spinach, defrosted
8 ozs. sea scallops
½ cup white wine
1 tbs. shallot, finely chopped
1 tbs. butter

Heat spinach pouch in boiling water or in the microwave. If the scallops are large, cut them in slices across the grain. Bring wine to a boil in a medium saucepan and poach scallops 2-3 minutes until just barely cooked. Remove scallops and drain. Add shallot to wine; boil rapidly until about 1 tbs. of wine remains in pan. Stir in butter. Place ½ creamed spinach in 2 au gratin dishes or 1 small baking dish. Arrange drained scallops over spinach and top with remaining spinach. Spoon shallot mixture over spinach. Broil for 2-3 minutes until dish is hot.

Steamed Mussels in Wine Sauce

Steamed mussels are easy to do and make a great first course or an intimate dinner.

4 dozen mussels, cleaned
2 tbs. olive oil
¼ tsp. hot pepper flakes
2 cloves garlic, chopped
1 cup white wine
1 tsp. oil
1 tsp. curry powder
1 small tomato, peeled, seeded, chopped
¼ cup heavy cream
salt and freshly ground pepper
1 tbs. parsley, finely chopped

Scrub mussel shells with a stiff brush and remove beards. Wash well. Heat olive oil in a large deep skillet or heavy pot. Add pepper flakes, garlic, mussels and wine. Cover pot and cook over high heat 3-4 minutes, or until shells have all opened. Shake pan occasionally while mussels are steaming. Remove mussels to a large serving bowl. Heat 1 tsp. oil in a small saucepan, add curry powder and cook over low heat 1-2 minutes to release flavor. Strain ¾ cup of mussel liquid through cheesecloth or a coffee filter into saucepan with curry. Add tomato pieces, cream, salt, pepper and parsley and heat for 2-3 minutes until hot. Pour over mussels and serve with small forks and lots of paper napkins.

Potatoes and Rice

Potatoes, substantial and hearty, are the side dish of choice among the men in our survey, and baked potatoes rank first with more than 80% of them. We've included a ''good-for-you'' version. Mashed potatoes ranked second, and we have a different version in **Mashed Potatoes Supreme**. And finally, to fill the bill for winner #3, we include **Classic Scalloped Potatoes**.

In the rice category, pilaf was the run-away favorite, with fried rice following. Here are some great new ways to fix old favorites.

Crisp Oven Wedges

Serves 2

Allow one medium potato for each person and expand this recipe to fit any number of people. You won't have any left no matter how many you do.

2 medium baking potatoes, scrubbed, skins left on
2 tbs. full-flavored olive oil
salt and freshly ground pepper
dash cayenne pepper **or** chili powder or cumin

Cut each potato in half and each half into 4 wedges. Line a cookie sheet with sides with aluminum foil. Pour olive oil on a large plate; add salt, pepper and cayenne. Dip each potato wedge in seasoned olive oil and place on cookie sheet. Bake at 400° for 30-35 minutes until potatoes are done and nicely browned. Serve immediately.

Grilled New Potatoes

Serves 2

These are simple to do when you are grilling steaks or chicken.

8-10 small new potatoes
1 tbs. olive oil
1 clove garlic, finely minced

salt and freshly ground pepper
dash cayenne **or** cumin

Scrub new potatoes, but do not peel. Place in a saucepan, cover with water and bring to a boil. Cook, covered, about 15 minutes, until potatoes are almost done. Remove to a plate covered with paper towels and drain. Heat olive oil in a small skillet and sauté garlic over low heat 1 minute. Add salt, pepper and cayenne. Coat cooked new potatoes with seasoned olive oil, thread on skewers or put in small barbecue basket. Place on grill and cook for about 10 minutes, turning once or twice, until skin is brown and crisp and potatoes are tender.

Variation: Use fresh or dried rosemary, thyme or oregano with olive oil in place of cayenne or cumin.

Classic Scalloped Potatoes

These potatoes are creamy and satisfying. Serve them with barbecued steaks, lamb chops or chicken. Or if you are a real potato lover, forget the meat.

2-2½ lbs. boiling potatoes, peeled
1-1¼ cups milk
1 tbs. butter
1 cup heavy cream
1 tsp. salt
freshly ground white pepper
1 tbs. butter
2 tbs. shallots, finely chopped
2 tbs. Parmesan cheese

Slice potatoes into ⅛" slices and pat very dry on paper towels. Heat milk in a large heavy saucepan over medium heat. Add potato slices, separating them as you put them in the milk. Bring milk to a boil, cover and simmer over low heat for about 10-15 minutes, or until milk has almost been completely absorbed. Check to see that milk in bottom of pan doesn't scorch. Add heavy cream, salt and pepper to potatoes and bring to a boil. Cover and simmer over very low heat for another 10-15 minutes until most of cream has been absorbed. Gently shift potato slices with a small spatula once or twice during cooking, taking care that bottom of pan doesn't burn. While the potatoes are cooking, sauté shallots in butter for 1-2 minutes and set aside. Butter a 12" x 12" x 2" ovenproof baking dish. Place cooked potatoes and shallots in dish, top with Parmesan cheese and run under a preheated broiler for 5-10 minutes until top is nicely browned.

Good-for-You Twice Baked Potatoes

Serves 4

This gives you the creamy taste of a rich potato dish with less fat.

4 large potatoes, baked
1 cup lowfat cottage cheese
½ cup lowfat milk
2 tbs. lowfat cream cheese
1 tsp. garlic powder

1 tsp. onion powder
dash nutmeg
freshly ground pepper
dash paprika
fresh parsley, chopped

With a mixer or using a wire whisk, blend cottage cheese with milk, cream cheese, garlic powder, onion powder, nutmeg and pepper until smooth. Meanwhile, cut hot potatoes in half. Scoop out potato pulp, being careful to leave skins in one piece for restuffing. Mix potato pulp with cottage cheese mixture. Heap mixture back into skins. Sprinkle with paprika and fresh parsley. Bake in a 375° oven just until hot and golden.

Simply Wonderful Potatoes

Serves 4

If he prefers one herb over another, simply substitute for the dill in this recipe to create a recipe just for him.

4 cups hot boiled potatoes, cubed
3-4 tbs. butter or margarine
1 tsp. dill
freshly ground pepper
½ tsp. salt
2-3 tbs. fresh parsley, chopped

In a medium bowl, combine potatoes and butter. Toss to coat well. Sprinkle with dill, pepper, salt and fresh parsley. Serve immediately.

Mashed Potatoes Supreme

Serves 4-6

This variation of common mashed potatoes makes a change.

4 large potatoes, peeled
1 (3 ozs.) pkg. cream cheese, softened
½ cup sour cream
1 tsp. onion powder
½ tsp. salt

freshly ground pepper
dash nutmeg
1 tbs. butter or margarine
½ cup grated cheddar
   cheese (optional)

In a medium saucepan, cook potatoes in salted water until done. Drain; mash until smooth with a masher or mixer. Add cream cheese, sour cream, onion powder, salt, pepper, nutmeg and butter. Top with cheddar cheese if desired. Spoon into a casserole and serve hot.

Skinny Spud Bake

Serves 6

Even men on special diets can enjoy this delicious creation.

2 cups potatoes, thinly sliced
½ cup mushrooms, sliced
½ cup onions, sliced
4 beef bouillon cubes
1 cup boiling water
¼ tsp. thyme leaves
dash pepper

In a nonstick 9" square baking pan sprayed with vegetable spray, combine potatoes, mushrooms and onions. Dissolve bouillon cubes in boiling water. Add thyme and pepper. Pour over vegetables. Cover and bake at 350° for 30 minutes. Uncover and bake 15 minutes more or until vegetables are tender. Only 55 calories per serving!

Tip: Use low salt beef bouillon cubes.

Orange Rice Pilaf

Serves 4-6

This is a delicious accompaniment for ham, turkey or roast pork, or use it to stuff pork chops.

4 tbs. butter
1 medium onion, finely chopped
1 cup uncooked rice
grated rind of 1 orange
juice of 2 oranges **plus** enough chicken broth to make 2¼ cups liquid
½ tsp. salt
1-2 tsp. **each** slivered almonds and white raisins

Melt butter in a large saucepan and sauté onion until soft but not brown. Add rice to pan; stir until rice is well coated with butter and becomes translucent, about 5 minutes. Add orange rind, orange juice with chicken broth and salt. Bring to a boil, cover and cook over very low heat about 20-25 minutes until rice is tender and liquid is absorbed. Stir in slivered almonds and raisins.

Baked Rice and Lentil Casserole

Serves 4

Lentils give this hearty dish a little bit of crunch. Serve with baked fish or roast chicken.

3 tbs. butter
1 small onion, chopped
½ tsp. cumin
½ cup lentils

1 cup uncooked long grain rice
1 (14 ozs.) can chicken broth
¾ cup water
salt and freshly ground pepper

Preheat oven to 375°. Melt butter in an ovenproof baking dish and sauté onion until soft but not browned. Stir in cumin and cook 2-3 minutes longer. Add lentils, rice, chicken stock, water, salt and pepper. Bring mixture to a boil, cover and bake at 375° for 20-25 minutes until liquid is absorbed and rice is tender.

Charlie's Monterey Rice

Serves 4

Charlie offers a zesty rice casserole to accompany barbecued hamburgers or steaks.

½ cup butter **or** margarine
1 tsp. oregano
2 cloves garlic, minced
2 tbs. fresh parsley, chopped
1 tsp. sweet basil, dried

1 small onion, diced
3-4 large tomatoes, peeled, seeded, chopped
3 cups cooked rice
¼ cup Parmesan cheese, grated
2 cups Monterey Jack cheese, shredded

In a large saucepan, melt butter with oregano, minced garlic and basil. Add onion and sauté until lightly browned. Add tomatoes and stir until hot and "saucy." Add parsley. In a lightly greased 2-quart casserole dish, mix together sauce, rice, Parmesan cheese and 1 cup Monterey Jack cheese. Spread remaining cup of cheese on top. Cover and bake at 350° for 20 minutes or until top is browned.

Perfect Rice

Serves 6

Here is a recipe for perfectly cooked, fluffy rice, each grain separate.

2½ cups uncooked long grain rice
3 tbs. salt
3 tbs. butter

Heat 4-6 quarts of water to boiling in a large kettle. Add salt and rice and boil vigorously, uncovered, for 15 minutes. Pour rice into strainer to drain and rinse with cold water. Melt butter in a large heavy saucepan. Stir in well drained rice. Wrap lid of saucepan with a dish towel so that towel is between lid and saucepan. Place over very low heat and steam 25 minutes without lifting lid. Remove from heat. Rice will wait until you are ready to serve it, or at least 1 hour. Toss lightly with a fork just before serving.

Tip: If using Basmati rice, decrease boiling time to 10 minutes.

Spinach Rice Bake

This was sent to us by Adrienne because her husband begs her for it. Think of the bargaining power! It might work for you.

3 cups cooked rice
¼ cup butter, melted
4 eggs, beaten
2 cups cheddar cheese, grated
1 cup milk
1 (10 ozs.) pkg. frozen chopped spinach, cooked, well drained

1 tbs. onion, chopped
1 tsp. Worcestershire sauce
2 tsp. salt
½ tsp. marjoram
½ tsp. thyme
½ tsp. rosemary

In a large mixing bowl, mix butter, eggs, cheese and milk. Add spinach, onion, Worcestershire sauce, salt, marjoram, thyme and rosemary. Stir in cooked rice. Pour into a lightly greased 2-quart baking dish and cover. Place dish in a pan of water and bake at 350° for 35 minutes.

Rice Pilaf

The perfect side dish for shish kebob.

3 (14 ozs. each) cans chicken broth
½ cup butter
½ cup fine dried egg noodles, crushed
2 cups uncooked long grain rice
finely ground white pepper

Bring chicken broth to a boil in a large saucepan. Melt 4 tbs. butter in a 3-quart flameproof casserole with a tightly fitting lid. Add crushed egg noodles to melted butter and stir until golden brown. Add boiling broth, rice and white pepper; stir gently. Boil 5 minutes. Cover casserole and bake 20-25 minutes in a 350° oven until all liquid is absorbed. Stir gently, dot with remaining butter, return to oven and bake uncovered for 5 minutes. Serve immediately.

Doc's Fried Rice

Here is Doc's version of man's second favorite rice dish. He likes it as a side dish and thinks it makes a great breakfast, too.

3 tbs. oil
2 eggs, lightly beaten
½ medium onion, chopped
½ green bell pepper, chopped
1½ cups cooked chicken **or** beef or pork, chopped
3 cups cold cooked rice
finely ground white pepper
2 tbs. soy sauce
¼ cup toasted slivered almonds
3-4 green onions, thinly sliced

Preheat a large skillet and add 1 tbs oil. Scramble eggs in oil, turning frequently and break into small pieces with a spatula. Remove to a plate. Add remaining oil, onion, green pepper and sauté 1-2 minutes to soften. Add meat and toss to coat with oil and heat through. Add rice, mix well, and sprinkle with pepper and soy sauce. Continue to cook until rice is heated through. Return scrambled eggs to pan and combine with rice. Turn out onto a heated platter, sprinkle with almonds and green onions and serve immediately.

Tips
- Rice that has been refrigerated for a day works best. Use fingers to break rice chunks into individual grains.
- To toast almonds, spread on a cookie sheet and bake at 350° for 5-10 minutes, stirring frequently to avoid burning.

Pasta

Pasta is high on the list of men's favorite dishes. Most men said they liked pasta of all kinds. Only a few were indifferent, and no one listed it as a food they disliked. One man's favorite pasta dish was Kraft Macaroni and Cheese. But these recipes, many offered by men who like to cook, top that one! Pasta is a satisfying, healthy food that can be served quickly and in many different ways with a wide variety of sauces, meats and vegetables. Here are some pasta dishes for you to try.

Spaghetti with Clam Sauce

Mike developed this sumptuous dish for his wife.

1 (6½ ozs.) can chopped clams
1 (6½ ozs.) can minced clams
4 tbs. butter
1 tbs. olive oil
1 large clove garlic, finely chopped
½ tsp. red pepper flakes
3 tbs. fresh parsley, chopped
1 (12 ozs.) pkg. spaghetti

In a frying pan, melt butter and add olive oil. Add garlic and red pepper flakes. Cook 1-2 minutes, being careful not to brown garlic. Meanwhile, cook spaghetti according to package directions. Add liquid from canned clams to butter-garlic mixture and heat through. When spaghetti is cooked, lift it out into a large heated serving bowl. Stir clams and parsley into butter mixture. Heat briefly. Pour over spaghetti. Do **not** serve with Parmesan cheese.

Tip: Always cook pasta in a large amount of boiling, salted water (about 6 qts. water and 2 tbs. salt per 1 lb. pasta), uncovered. Fresh pasta cooks in 2-3 minutes, commercial dried pasta in about 8 minutes. Do not overcook. Pasta should be firm to the bite, but not too chewy. Periodically pull out a strand and bite it to check on doneness. Do not rinse pasta that is to be served hot. Save a few tablespoons of pasta-cooking water to add to sauce if pasta seems dry after being sauced.

Artichoke and Tomato Fettucine

Serves 4-6

Anthony created this extra-nice pasta dish.

1 lb. fettucine
1 cup fresh mushrooms, sliced
1 tbs. butter **or** margarine
1 can cream of mushroom soup
½ cup milk
½ cup Parmesan cheese, grated

1 tsp. dried oregano
1 tbs. parsley, chopped
½ tsp. white pepper
1 (6 ozs.) jar marinated artichoke
    hearts, drained
1 pint cherry tomatoes, halved, seeded

Cook fettucine according to package directions. In a large saucepan, sauté mushrooms in butter. Add soup and milk and heat just to boiling. Add Parmesan cheese, oregano, parsley and pepper. Drain artichoke hearts. Add artichokes and halved tomatoes to soup mixture. Add all to drained noodles. Toss until well coated. Pour into a heated serving dish and serve immediately.

Labor of Love Spaghetti Sauce

Serves 8-10

Paul stepped in to cook when his wife went back to work. This recipe is one of the results.

2 lbs. bone-in chuck steak
2 tbs. virgin olive oil
1 cup onion, chopped
1 cup fresh parsley, chopped
2 cloves garlic, minced
1 cup fresh mushrooms, sliced
2 (28 ozs. each) cans whole tomatoes with juice

1 (6 ozs.) can tomato paste
2 tsp. salt
3 tsp. oregano
½ tsp. rosemary
½ tsp. thyme

Slice steak into 2" x 1" strips and brown in olive oil in a large skillet. Combine remaining ingredients in a refrigerator container and refrigerate overnight. The next morning transfer to crock pot and cook on low heat 10-12 hours, or 5-6 hours on high heat. Serve over cooked spaghetti or noodles.

Veggie Lasagna

Joe is a successful man who is handsome, health-conscious and Italian. This is one of his best dishes.

9 wide lasagna noodles

Filling:
1 (10 ozs.) pkg. frozen spinach, thawed
2 tbs. Parmesan cheese, grated
1 cup cottage cheese
¼ tsp. nutmeg
½ cup cheddar cheese, shredded
½ cup Monterey Jack cheese, shredded
freshly ground pepper

Sauce:
2 tbs. olive oil
2 cloves garlic, minced
½ cup onion, chopped
½ lb. fresh mushrooms, sliced
2 cups tomato sauce
½ tsp. basil
½ tsp. oregano
¼ cup Parmesan cheese, grated

In a medium bowl, mix spinach, Parmesan cheese, cottage cheese, nutmeg, cheddar cheese, Jack cheese and pepper. Set aside. In a medium skillet, sauté garlic, onion and mushrooms in olive oil. Add tomato sauce, basil and oregano. Simmer 20 minutes. Cook noodles according to package directions, undercooking just slightly. In a lightly greased 9" x 13" glass pan, spread 4 tbs. sauce on bottom and then layer noodles, filling and sauce. Top with ¼ cup Parmesan cheese. Bake at 350° for 30 minutes or until lasagna bubbles around edges.

Mushroom Gorgonzola Pasta

Serves 3-4

Rich and delicious for men who really love the assertive flavor of blue cheese in a creamy pasta dish.

1 lb. pasta, cooked, hot
2-3 tbs. butter
2 cloves garlic, finely chopped
dash red pepper flakes

½ lb. mushrooms, sliced
½ cup heavy cream
4 ozs. Gorgonzola cheese, cubed
2 tbs. parsley, chopped

In a medium skillet, melt butter and sauté garlic, red pepper flakes and mushrooms. Add cream and simmer 2-3 minutes, stirring occasionally. Add cubed cheese and hot pasta and toss. Sprinkle with parsley and serve.

Spaghetti Carbonara

Serves 4-5

Here is a classic pasta sauce with bacon, eggs and cream. If it is available, the Italian rolled "bacon" called pancetta will add special character and flavor to this dish.

1 lb. fresh pasta **or** 12 ozs. dried
½ lb. bacon **or** pancetta
1 large onion, chopped
½ cup parsley, finely chopped
2 eggs, room temperature

¾ cup Parmesan cheese, freshly grated
¼ tsp. hot pepper flakes
½ cup heavy cream
2 tbs. full-flavored olive oil for pasta

Bring pasta water to a boil while you are preparing sauce. Cut bacon into 1" pieces. Sauté in a skillet until crisp. Remove bacon pieces and pour off all but 2 tbs. bacon fat from skillet. Sauté onion 3-4 minutes until soft. Combine parsley, eggs, Parmesan cheese, pepper flakes and cream in a small bowl. Cook pasta and drain well. Toss pasta with olive oil in a large warm bowl. Quickly pour egg mixture over hot pasta and mix. Add bacon and onion; toss with pasta. Serve immediately on warm plates.

Pasta with Pepperoni and
Mushroom Sauce

This is a quick hearty sauce when you are hungry and short on time.

12 ozs. fresh pasta **or** 8 ozs. dried pasta
1 tbs. oil
¼ lb. pepperoni, skin removed, thinly sliced
½ lb. fresh mushrooms, thinly sliced
4-5 green onions, sliced
½ cup heavy cream

While pasta is cooking, heat oil in a large skillet. Sauté pepperoni 3-4 minutes, remove and reserve. Add sliced mushrooms and onions to skillet. Sauté 4-5 minutes over medium heat until mushrooms are cooked and onions are soft. Add cream and pepperoni and heat through. Combine with hot, well-drained pasta and serve immediately on warm plates.

Pasta with Pesto Sauce

Fragrant fresh sweet basil leaves, garlic, walnuts or pine nuts and olive oil make a delicious quick pasta sauce.

1 lb. fresh pasta **or** 12 ozs. dried pasta
2 cups fresh basil leaves
3 large cloves garlic
¾ cup walnut pieces **or** pine nuts

¾ cup full-flavored olive oil
¾ cup Parmesan cheese,
  freshly grated
salt and freshly ground pepper

While pasta is cooking, place fresh basil leaves, garlic, nuts and olive oil in food processor bowl or blender container. Process until ingredients are well mixed, scraping down sides of container once or twice. Process until mixture is fairly smooth. Pour into a bowl and stir in cheese, salt and pepper. Toss with hot, drained pasta in a warm bowl.

Pasta Primavera

Use colorful fresh vegetables with pasta for a delicious good-for-you dinner.

12 ozs. fresh **or** 8 ozs. dried tagliarini, spaghetti or fettuccine
2 medium tomatoes, peeled, seeded, chopped
4 tbs. full-flavored olive oil
1 small onion, finely chopped
¼ tsp. red pepper flakes
½ lb. mushrooms, thinly sliced
1 clove garlic, minced
1 cup asparagus **or** green beans, diagonally sliced
1 cup carrots, coarsely grated
1 cup cauliflower pieces
½ cup fresh blanched **or** frozen peas
1 medium yellow squash, thinly sliced
1 medium red **or** green bell pepper, peeled and cut into thin strips
salt and freshly ground pepper
3 tbs. parsley, finely chopped
⅓ cup Parmesan cheese, grated

Time pasta so it is cooked when the sauce is finished. Heat olive oil in a large skillet. Sauté onion and red pepper flakes for 3-4 minutes. Add mushrooms and garlic and cook for 2 minutes over medium high heat. Add asparagus pieces, cauliflower pieces, yellow squash and peppers. Cover and cook 2 minutes. Add carrots, peas, salt and pepper; mix well. Toss with hot, well-drained pasta. Top with parsley and grated Parmesan cheese. Serve immediately on warm plates.

Jumbo Shells Stuffed with Chicken

Serves 4

This is an easy dish featuring a cooked chicken filling and a delicious Gruyere and sherry sauce for a special dinner.

8 ozs. jumbo shells

Chicken Filling:
1½ cups cooked chicken, cubed
½ cup pecans, coarsely chopped
4 tbs. parsley, finely chopped
1 egg
1 cup ricotta cheese
3 tbs. Parmesan cheese, grated
salt and freshly ground white pepper

Gruyere and Sherry Sauce:
2 tbs. butter
¼ cup shallots, minced
3 tbs. flour
1¼ cups chicken broth
¼ cup dry sherry
salt and freshly ground white pepper
½ cup Gruyere **or** Swiss cheese, grated
¼ cup heavy cream
Parmesan cheese for topping

Cook shells as directed on package. Drain and rinse with cold water and set aside. Combine chicken filling ingredients and stuff cooked shells with mixture. To make sauce: melt butter in a small saucepan, stir in shallots and cook 1 minute. Add flour and cook 2 minutes. Gradually add chicken broth and sherry; cook over low heat, stirring constantly until sauce thickens. Remove from heat and stir in salt, pepper, grated cheese and cream. Spoon over filled shells, sprinkle with Parmesan cheese and bake for 10-15 minutes until heated through. Place under the broiler to brown lightly. Serve immediately.

Manicotti

Cheese and ham filled manicotti shells are topped with a zesty tomato sauce. Serve with a crisp salad and hot garlic bread.

8 manicotti shells **or** Stuff-a-Roni shells

Filling:
½ lb. mozzarella cheese, grated
8 ozs. ricotta cheese
salt and freshly ground pepper
1 egg
½ cup ham, diced

Tomato Sauce:
1 (15 ozs.) can tomato sauce with tomato pieces
⅓ cup red wine
salt and freshly ground pepper
1½ tsp. Italian herb seasoning
1 garlic clove, minced
2 tbs. full-flavored olive oil
6-8 fresh mushrooms, thinly sliced

Cook manicotti shells according to package directions. Drain and rinse with cold water for easier handling. Set aside while preparing filling and sauce. Combine filling ingredients in a small bowl. Fill cooked manicotti shells using a small spoon. To make sauce: combine tomato sauce, wine, salt, pepper, Italian seasoning and garlic in a small saucepan. Simmer 20-25 minutes to blend flavors. Heat oil in a small skillet and sauté fresh mushrooms 4-5 minutes over high heat. Add mushrooms to cooked sauce. Pour tomato sauce over stuffed manicotti shells. Heat in a 350° oven for 15 minutes, or until hot and bubbly.

Vegetables and Soups

The men in our survey liked almost all vegetables, but corn was the all-out victor, and "on the cob" scored as the spirited 90% favorite. So naturally we include corn tips. Brussels sprouts often appeared on the "Foods I Dislike List," but even more often were listed as favorite. Other most disliked veggies included beets, lima beans and rutabaga. But many men seem to be adventurous, even listing such vegetables as eggplant and okra. And they all said, fresh, fresh, fresh!

We've discovered that men not only enjoy eating soup but many men listed soup as a favorite item to cook for family and friends. Robust and hearty were the words used to describe high scoring varieties men like to eat and like to cook. Here are some hearty choices for you to try.

Corn Tips

Buying Corn
- Husks should be clean, green and not dry.
- Silk tassles should be bright and golden with no signs of dampness.
- Kernels should be plump and glossy in rows that are well filled.
- Cook corn the same day you buy or pick it. The fresher the corn, the sweeter and more tender.

Cooking Corn
- Cold water method: place corn in a deep skillet without crowding. Cover with cold water. Cover skillet, bring to a boil, remove from heat, drain corn and serve immediately.
- Hot water method: bring a large pot of water to a boil. Add a little milk or sugar, but do not add salt. (Salt toughens corn.) Place cleaned corn into boiling water. Do not crowd. Cover. Cook 2-3 minutes, drain corn and serve immediately.
- Microwave method: place each ear of cleaned corn on waxed paper or on dampened paper towels. Brush ears with butter and twist ends of wrapping closed. Place on a microwave dish and microwave at full power according to individual oven directions: 2½ to 5 minutes for 1 ear, 5-7½ minutes for 2.
- Grilled-in-husks method: pull husks back, leaving husks attached at stem. Remove all silk. Butter ears. Recover ears with husks. Using string, tie ends closed. Soak in cold water 10 minutes. Grill over hot coals 15-20 minutes, turning often. Carefully remove husks, protecting hands with mitts.
- Grilled-in-foil method: butter cleaned, husked ears of corn. Wrap each ear loosely in heavy-duty aluminum foil. Grill over hot coals 15-20 minutes, turning ears every 5-6 minutes.

Buttering Corn
- Fill a jar about ¾ full of hot water. Add ½ cup butter and let it melt. The butter will rise to the top. Using tongs, dip each ear of corn in the jar and bring it out, buttered.
- Use a pastry brush to butter corn.
- Use a slice of buttered bread to butter corn.

Bobby ▶

Sandwiches, etc. (page 147) and Oatmeal Cookies (page 167)

Corn-Spinach Casserole

Serves 4-6

This tasty casserole will please that special man in your life, or 4-6 of them, if you have that many!

½ medium onion, chopped
¼ cup butter
1 (17 ozs.) can creamed corn
1 (10 ozs.) pkg. frozen chopped
    spinach, thawed, well drained
¼ tsp. dry mustard
dash nutmeg

2 tsp. cider vinegar
salt and freshly ground pepper
⅓ cup dry seasoned bread crumbs
1 tsp. parsley flakes
2 tbs. Parmesan cheese, grated
¼ cup Monterey Jack cheese, grated

In a medium skillet, melt 2 tbs. of the butter and sauté onion. Mix with corn, spinach, mustard, nutmeg, vinegar, salt and pepper. Turn into a greased, shallow baking dish. Melt remaining butter and mix with bread crumbs, parsley and cheeses. Sprinkle over vegetables and bake at 400° for 15 minutes or until golden and bubbly.

Garlic-Flavored Carrot Sticks

Serves 4

These flavorful carrot matchsticks keep in the refrigerator for a week and make a colorful addition to any dinner plate.

3 large carrots, about ½ lb.
2 tbs. full-flavored olive oil
1 large clove garlic, smashed

1 tbs. red wine vinegar
¼ tsp. oregano
salt and lots of freshly ground pepper

Peel carrots and cut into 2" long matchsticks. Bring approximately 4 cups of water to a boil in a saucepan. Cook carrots in boiling water 3-4 minutes until crisp tender. Drain and rinse with cold water. Heat olive oil and sauté garlic 2-3 minutes to release flavor. Remove garlic and discard. Place carrots in a bowl and while still warm, toss with olive oil, vinegar, oregano, salt and pepper. If storing in the refrigerator, stir occasionally to distribute marinade evenly.

◀ **Kevin**
Veggie Supreme Pita (page 149)

Crisp Marinated Cucumbers

2 cups

These cucumbers are a great side dish for grilled steaks or hamburgers, or as part of an antipasto plate. They keep well for at least a week in the refrigerator, if they last that long.

1 medium (8 ozs.) cucumber, **or**
  ½ European hothouse cucumber
½ large mild white onion
⅓ cup cider vinegar

½ tsp. salt
1 tsp. sugar
dash of Tabasco sauce
water (about ⅔ cup)

Peel cucumber with a vegetable peeler and score lengthwise with fork tines to a depth of ⅛". Use 2mm slicer blade on the food processor or slice thinly by hand. Cut peeled onion in half across the grain and slice each half the same thickness as cucumbers. Place in a glass jar with a lid and add vinegar, salt, sugar and hot sauce. Shake well to mix. Add just enough water to cover. Allow to mellow in the refrigerator for a day before serving.

Asparagus with Lemon Crumbs

Serves 3-4

Piquant lemon-flavored crumbs give asparagus a new delicious taste. This is particularly good with fish or roast chicken. He'll be so happy he'll chase you around the kitchen! For more asparagus!

1 lb. asparagus
2 tbs. butter
2-3 tbs. fresh bread crumbs

grated lemon rind from 1 lemon
salt and freshly ground pepper

Cook asparagus and drain well. Just before asparagus is done, melt butter in a small skillet. Add bread crumbs and sauté until crumbs are light brown. Watch carefully, because once they start to turn color, they get brown very fast. Stir in lemon rind, salt and pepper. Remove from heat and spoon over drained asparagus. Serve immediately.

Glazed Carrots

Serves 4-5

Carrots were #2 on the favorite vegetable list. This glazed carrot recipe is a special way of serving them.

6 carrots, cut into ovals
1 tbs. butter
2 tbs. honey

salt
⅛ tsp. ground ginger
¼ cup peach liqueur **or** apricot

In a saucepan, cook carrots in just enough water to barely cover. Cook until crisp tender. Add butter, honey, salt, ginger and liqueur. Stir and simmer until liquid has evaporated and carrots are nicely glazed.

Chinese Green Beans

Serves 4

Robert gives a new look and a new taste to green beans.

1 lb. tender young green beans, stemmed, cut into 1" pieces
¼ lb. lean ground pork
1 clove garlic, minced
¼ cup chicken stock
finely ground white pepper
½ tsp. cornstarch dissolved in 1 tbs. water
1 tbs. soy sauce
1 tbs. dry sherry

Heat a large skillet over medium heat and add pork. Stir pork and crumble with a spatula as pork browns. Add garlic and cook for a minute to soften. Add green beans, chicken stock and pepper; mix. Bring to a boil, cover pan and simmer 5-7 minutes until beans are crisp tender. In a small bowl, mix together cornstarch dissolved in water, soy sauce and sherry. Remove cover and stir in cornstarch mixture a few drops at a time until sauce is the consistency of heavy cream and glazes beans. Serve immediately.

Simply Divine Broccoli

Serves 4-6

This is a different way to serve one of men's favorites.

2 (10 ozs. each) pkgs. frozen broccoli spears, **or** 2 bunches fresh, trimmed into 2" pieces
1 (10½ ozs.) can cream of mushroom soup

2 tbs. white wine
1 tsp. Worcestershire sauce
¼ cup seasoned bread crumbs
¼ cup Parmesan cheese, grated

Partially cook broccoli in salted water. In a small bowl, combine mushroom soup, white wine and Worcestershire sauce. In a lightly greased casserole, layer broccoli and sauce, ending with sauce. Mix bread crumbs and Parmesan cheese together and sprinkle over broccoli. Bake at 350° for 20-25 minutes or until bubbly.

Broccoli Stir-Fry

Serves 2-3

Hot red pepper and garlic give a lift to this quick broccoli dish. This is a great side dish for barbecued meat or roast chicken.

10-12 ozs. broccoli flowerettes (1 large bunch)
1 tbs. olive oil
1 clove garlic, minced

⅛ tsp. hot red pepper flakes
⅓-½ cup water
salt and freshly ground pepper
1 tsp. sesame oil

Cut broccoli flowerettes into equal sized pieces using about 1" of stem. Heat oil in a medium sized nonstick skillet over medium heat. Add broccoli, stirring gently to coat with oil. Add garlic, red pepper flakes, salt, pepper and ⅓ cup water. Cover, lower heat and cook for about 5 minutes. Check to see if there is enough liquid in pan so broccoli does not burn, adding more water if necessary. Continue to cook until broccoli is crisp tender, or to your taste. The water should have evaporated at this point. Sprinkle broccoli with sesame oil and place in a serving dish. Serve hot or at room temperature.

Baked Eggplant Casserole

This dish is easy to do in the microwave and is great by itself or as a filling for stuffed peppers or tomatoes.

2 tbs. full-flavored olive oil
½ cup onion, coarsely chopped
2 cloves garlic, minced
½ lb. eggplant, unpeeled, diced in ½" pieces
1 red pepper, cut into thin strips
1 tsp. fresh thyme leaves, **or** ½ tsp. dried
1 small zucchini, cut in half lengthwise, thinly sliced
hot pepper flakes
salt and freshly ground pepper

Place olive oil, onion, garlic, eggplant, red pepper strips and thyme in a 2-quart microwave casserole. Cover and cook on high 3 minutes. Uncover; add zucchini, hot pepper flakes, salt and pepper. Stir well, recover and cook another 2 minutes. Let stand covered for another minute. Serve hot.

Variation: Add some cooked, sliced Italian sausage or chunks of ham for a more hearty dish. Or add fresh, peeled, seeded and chopped tomato pieces after mixture has cooled.

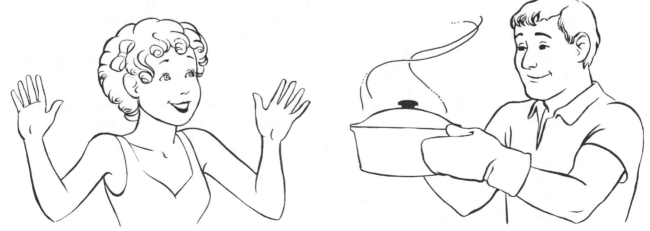

Dutch Split Pea Soup

Serves 8

Mike says this soup should be so thick that a spoon will stand upright in it!

9 cups water
1 lb. dried green split peas
1 lb. ham, cut into ½" cubes
3 leeks, carefully washed, thinly sliced
4 stalks celery with leaves, thinly sliced
2 cloves garlic, chopped

¾ tsp. crushed dried savory leaves
1½ tsp. salt
½ tsp. pepper
½ lb. cooked smoked sausage
  (Kielbasa, knockwurst)

In a large Dutch oven, bring water and peas to a boil and boil 2 minutes. Remove from heat, cover and let stand 1 hour. Add remaining ingredients except sausage to peas. Bring to a boil, reduce heat, cover and simmer 2 hours. Add sausage to soup, cover and simmer until sausage is hot, 10-15 minutes. Serve soup hot; remove sausage, slice and serve with rye or pumpernickel bread and mustard.

Paul's Curried Pea Soup

Serves 4

Beautifully green, this thick and creamy soup makes a great first course; or serve it with a salad and hot French bread for lunch or a light supper.

1 tbs. butter
½ cup onion, finely chopped
½ tsp. curry powder
1 (10 ozs.) pkg. frozen green peas,
  defrosted

1 tbs. flour
2 (14 ozs. each) cans chicken broth
1 cup milk
salt and finely ground white pepper
sour cream for garnish

Melt butter in a heavy saucepan over medium heat. Sauté onion for 2-3 minutes until translucent. Stir in curry powder and cook for another minute. Add peas and stir to coat with butter. Sprinkle with flour and stir. Add chicken broth and bring to a boil, lower heat and simmer for 5 minutes. Pour into a blender container or food processor bowl and process until very smooth. Return soup to pan, add milk, salt and pepper and heat. Adjust for seasoning and serve immediately with a dollop of sour cream for garnish.

Clam Chowder

Clam chowder is always popular with men. Here is a good, fast recipe.

1 tbs. butter
1 cup onion, chopped
½ cup celery, chopped
3½ cups milk
salt and freshly ground pepper

6-8 drops Tabasco
½ cup instant potato flakes **or** 1½ cups
  leftover mashed potatoes
2 (6½ ozs. each) cans minced clams

In a medium pan, melt butter and sauté onion and celery. Add milk, salt, pepper and Tabasco. Just before serving, add instant potato flakes or mashed potatoes. Heat until thick. Add minced clams. Strain clam juice through a paper towel or coffee filter to avoid making soup sandy, and add to soup. Serve hot.

Potato Corn Soup

This satisfying soup will make him warm on a cold day.

1 (14 ozs.) can chicken broth
3 medium potatoes, peeled, cubed
⅓ cup onion, chopped
1 tsp. salt
⅛ tsp. nutmeg
2 cups half-and-half **or** milk

1 (6 ozs.) can sliced water chestnuts,
  rinsed, drained
1 (10½ ozs.) can whole kernel corn,
  undrained
fresh chopped parsley for garnish

In a medium saucepan, place broth, potatoes, onion, salt and nutmeg, adding enough water to cover potatoes, if necessary. Simmer, covered, about 15 minutes, or until potatoes are tender. Add half-and-half. Bring to simmer; add water chestnuts and corn. Serve hot, sprinkled with fresh parsley.

Variation: Add 1 (6½ ozs.) can minced clams, undrained, or 1 cup cooked chicken or turkey.

Lentil Soup

This thick, hearty, stick-to-the-ribs kind of soup keeps well in the refrigerator for several days. It tastes better the next day — add 1 cup of cooked macaroni shells when you reheat it.

¼ lb. bacon, diced
1 medium onion, chopped
2 large carrots, chopped
4 stalks celery, chopped
1 cup lentils, washed in cold water
¼ cup flour

1 cup potatoes, peeled, cubed
1 tbs. parsley, chopped
6 cups beef broth **or** 2 tbs. beef base,
    dissolved in 6 cups hot water
dash nutmeg
1 ham hock

In a large Dutch oven, sauté bacon; add onion, carrot and celery. Wash lentils and mix with flour until well coated. Add to bacon and vegetables and gently sauté. Add parsley, beef broth, nutmeg and ham hock. Simmer 2½ hours. Add potatoes and simmer 30 minutes more. Makes 4-6 servings.

Hamburger Vegetable Soup

This is an old favorite.

1 lb. lean ground beef
1-2 tbs. vegetable oil
1 medium onion, chopped
2 cloves garlic, minced
3 cups hot water **or** bouillon
6 fresh tomatoes, chopped **or**
    1 (28 ozs.) can stewed tomatoes with juice
1 cup carrots, chopped
1 cup celery, chopped

1 cup potatoes, chopped
½ cup mushrooms, sliced
½ tsp. Italian seasoning
1 bay leaf
pinch of basil
1-2 tsp. salt
½ tsp pepper
1 tsp. Worcestershire sauce

In a heavy kettle or Dutch oven, brown beef. Add onions and garlic; cook until onions are translucent. Drain fat. Add water or bouillon. Add tomatoes, carrots, celery, potato and mushrooms. Add seasonings. Stir and simmer 30 minutes or until vegetables are tender.

Steve's Tortilla Soup

Here is a spicy soup Steve first tasted in Mexico City and recreated for you.

1 dozen corn tortillas, cut into 1" strips
oil for frying
2 tbs. oil
1 onion, chopped
4 fresh Jalapeno peppers, seeded, membrane removed, thinly sliced
4 cloves garlic, finely chopped
2 (16 ozs. each) cans chopped tomatoes with juice
4 cups chicken broth
1 tsp. cumin
1 tsp. freshly ground black pepper
¼ cup fresh cilantro, chopped
salt to taste
sour cream and fresh cilantro for garnish

Fry tortilla strips in ¼" oil in a large frying pan until crisp. Drain on paper towels. Sauté onions, Jalapeno peppers and garlic in oil until onions are translucent. Blend onion mixture and tomatoes in a blender until smooth. Mix chicken broth, cumin, pepper and cilantro with tomato mixture in a large saucepan. Heat to boiling, add ½ of the fried tortilla strips and heat 1 minute. Place remaining tortilla strips into 6 soup bowls, breaking them into 2-3 pieces. Ladle soup into bowls and garnish with a dollop of sour cream and a sprig of fresh cilantro.

Breads and Sandwiches

What's better than bread, to complete a meal or, with filling, to make a meal? In the sandwich department, men liked the old favorites, but first was turkey, then roast beef, followed by tuna, Reuben, hamburger and club. And one man listed his favorite: "Whatever's in the 'Fridge Sandwich." Along with some good sandwich ideas, we've added several breads and some ideas for French bread and spreads.

Sweet Breakfast Treats

These are cake-like muffins with a sweet cinnamon-spice crust.

⅓ cup butter, softened
½ cup sugar
1 egg
1 tsp. vanilla
1½ cups all-purpose flour
1½ tsp. baking powder

½ tsp. salt
¼ tsp. nutmeg
½ cup milk
1 tsp. cinnamon
⅓ cup brown sugar, packed
⅓ cup pecans, chopped

In a medium bowl, mix butter, sugar, egg and vanilla until light and fluffy. In a second bowl, mix flour, baking powder, salt and nutmeg. Add dry ingredients alternately with milk to butter mixture just until blended. Fill greased or paper lined muffin cups ⅔ full. In a small bowl, mix cinnamon, brown sugar and pecans. Sprinkle some of mixture on top of muffin batter in each cup. Bake at 350° for 20 minutes.

Parmesan Pull-Apart

This is crusty and delicious, and so easy you won't believe it. Add a hearty soup and a plate of crunchy raw vegetables and you have a perfect supper or lunch.

2 (1 lb. each) loaves frozen bread dough
¼-½ cup butter **or** margarine, melted
1 cup Parmesan cheese, grated

Thaw dough according to directions. With nonstick vegetable spray, spray a bundt pan or tube pan (or two loaf pans). Cut each loaf into 12 equal pieces. Dip each piece of dough first into melted butter, then into cheese. Place pieces of dough in pan. Cover with a clean towel and allow to rise until double in size, about 1 hour. Bake at 350° for 30-35 minutes or until golden and loaf sounds hollow when tapped. Remove from pan immediately and cool on a wire rack.

Cheese Bread

This bread is not for calorie counters, but it's worth it.

2 cups cheddar cheese, grated
½ cup mayonnaise
1 bunch green onions, chopped
1 loaf French bread, sliced in half lengthwise

In a medium bowl, mix grated cheese, mayonnaise and green onion. Spread thickly on both halves of bread. Wrap in foil and bake in a 400° oven 20 minutes. Open foil and turn oven to broil. Watch carefully until cheese bubbles. Remove from oven and cut into pieces.

Spreads for French Bread

Use the baking instructions from **Cheese Bread** with any of these combinations spread on French bread.

- **Garlic Spread**. Mix together ½ cup butter or margarine, ⅛ tsp. garlic powder and ½ tsp. dry mustard.
- **Dill Butter**. Mix together ½ cup butter or margarine and ½ tsp. dill.
- **Sweet Basil Butter**. Mix together ½ cup butter or margarine and ½ tsp. dried basil or 1 tbs. fresh chopped basil.
- **Chili Spread**. Mix together ½ cup butter or margarine and 1 tbs. taco seasoning mix.
- **Maple Butter**. Mix together ½ cup butter or margarine and 1 tbs. real maple syrup.
- **Cinnamon Spice Butter**. Mix together ½ cup butter or margarine, ½ tsp. cinnamon, ¼ tsp. nutmeg and 1 tbs. honey.

Beer Bread

This bread is a snap to mix up in a jiffy, and if there are any leftovers, makes wonderful toast. Your hunk will love it.

3 cups self-rising flour
3 tbs. sugar
12 ozs. beer
2 tbs. butter, melted

In a medium bowl, gently mix flour, sugar and beer just until blended. Do not overmix. Turn into a lightly greased 9" x 5" x 3" loaf pan. Bake at 350° for 1 hour and 15 minutes. Drizzle top with melted butter. Serve warm.

Monte Cristo Sandwich

This delicious old friend isn't so common anymore, but it's a real man's sandwich, and worth reviving.

4 slices bread, crusts removed
1 egg
¼ cup milk
salt and freshly ground pepper
4 thin slices of assorted lunch meat (turkey,
    chicken, ham, salami or other)
2 thin slices Swiss cheese
thin slices of kosher dill pickle
Dijon mustard
butter or margarine for frying

Beat eggs, milk, salt and pepper together in a shallow dish. Dip bread slices in batter, drain and place on waxed paper. Spread 2 slices of bread with mustard and arrange lunch meat, cheese and dill pickle on each half. Cover with remaining bread slices and fry, in butter, in a medium hot skillet until brown. Serve immediately.

Cheese Stix

These rate a hug. Serve them with soup or a salad. The trick to easy preparation is to freeze the bread.

one loaf white bread, unsliced
½ cup butter or margarine, room temperature
1 (5 ozs.) jar sharp processed cheese, room temperature
1 egg white

Freeze bread for 1 hour. Trim off crusts. Cut into 3 lengthwise slices; cut through all slices, making strips about ¾" wide. Arrange on a greased cookie sheet 1" apart and return to freezer. Beat egg white slightly. Add softened butter and cheese. Remove strips from freezer, several at a time, and spread mixture on all sides of bread; return to freezer. When ready, bake at 325° for 15-20 minutes, until golden brown and crunchy.

Mike's Reuben Sandwich

Serves 6

Reuben sandwiches are a traditional favorite, and this is Mike's version for a group.

1 (12 ozs.) can sauerkraut, drained
12 slices rye bread
Thousand Island dressing
½ lb. corned beef, thinly sliced
½ lb. Swiss cheese, thinly sliced
margarine
pickle spears

Heat sauerkraut. Spread Thousand Island dressing on each slice of bread. Evenly layer 6 bread slices with corned beef, sauerkraut and Swiss cheese. Top sandwiches with remaining bread slices. Spread outside of bread with margarine and grill sandwiches in 2 skillets, pressing down firmly with a spatula. Grill both sides until cheese is melted and corned beef is warm. Serve with kosher dill pickle spears.

Sandwiches, Sandwiches, Sandwiches

Try these ideas on your special man and see what he thinks. Some are whole sandwiches and some are just spreads. Because peanut butter was a frequently listed favorite, we've included a few extra peanut butter ideas.

- Mashed canned or leftover beans, mustard, chopped onion and chopped pickle on rye bread.
- Finely chopped green pepper and cream cheese.
- Green pepper and onions sautéed in olive oil, added to scrambled eggs. Serve on French roll.
- Refried beans mixed with cooked ground beef, seasoned with chili powder, in a warm tortilla.
- Finely chopped dried or chipped beef mixed with cream cheese and sweet pickle relish on whole wheat bread.
- Grated cheddar cheese moistened with mayonnaise, with hamburger relish on whole grain bread. Could also use as a spread for ham sandwiches.
- Meat loaf, sliced tomato, lettuce, onion and pickle with mustard on sour dough bread.
- Leftover chicken, chopped celery, onion, slivered toasted almonds, seedless grape halves, mayonnaise and curry served on a split croissant.
- Peanut butter, apple butter and chopped nuts.
- Peanut butter topped with orange slices and sprinkled with toasted coconut.
- Peanut butter, onion slices and dill pickle slices.
- Peanut butter and horseradish.
- Deviled ham mixed with mayonnaise, Dijon mustard and chopped onion or horseradish.
- Chopped chicken salad, cashew nuts, mayonnaise and curry powder.
- Cream cheese and horseradish.
- Cream cheese flavored with anchovy paste, mixed with chopped toasted almonds.
- Grated sharp cheddar, sweet pickle and mayonnaise.
- Grated sharp cheddar, port wine and mayonnaise.
- Liverwurst, mayonnaise and chopped pecans.

Grilled Turkey Melt

Serves 2

Turkey sandwiches were #1. Here's one version.

4 slices sour dough bread
1 tbs. mayonnaise
½-1 tsp. Dijon mustard
sliced turkey
sliced Swiss cheese
1 small green apple, pared, thinly sliced
butter or margarine

Spread sour dough bread with mixture of mayonnaise and mustard. Cover 2 pieces of bread with turkey and Swiss cheese. Add a layer of thinly sliced apple. Cover with another piece of bread. Spread top slices of bread with butter or margarine and place sandwiches butter side down in a medium hot frying pan. Butter second pieces of bread; turn when bottoms become golden brown.

Tuna Salad Melt

Serves 2

Tuna is a frequent choice, according to our surveys. Try this variation on the theme.

1 can tuna, drained, flaked
2-3 tbs. mayonnaise
2 green onions, chopped
1 stalk celery, chopped

4 slices cheddar cheese
4 slices tomato
2 English muffins, halved

Mix together tuna, mayonnaise, green onion and celery. Spread on English muffin halves. Add a slice of cheddar cheese and a slice of tomato to each half and broil until tuna is hot and cheese is melted.

Variation: Substitute Swiss cheese for cheddar and rye bread for English muffins.

Veggie Supreme Pita

Serves 1

A vegetable special makes a wholesome sandwich change.

1 pita pocket, cut into 2 pieces
2 tsp. mayonnaise
1 small tomato, sliced
4 slices onion
1 oz. Monterey Jack cheese, sliced
2 tbs. sprouts
1 small avocado, sliced

Spread the inside of each pita pocket half with mayonnaise. Tuck tomato, onion and cheese slices into pockets. Top with sprouts and avocado slices.

French Bread Pizza

Serves 4

If you don't want the task of making pizza crust, but love pizza (and we bet that man in your life does), here's a terrific way to do your own pizzas at home.

1 loaf French bread, split in half
1 (14 ozs.) jar pizza sauce
½ tsp. dried basil
1 tsp. dried parsley
¼ tsp. garlic powder
1-2 cups pepperoni, thinly sliced (½-¾ lb.)
1 cup fresh mushrooms, thinly sliced
2 cups mozzarella cheese, shredded

Place bread halves on a cookie sheet, cut side up. Toast under broiler, being careful not to burn. Spread each half with pizza sauce. Sprinkle with basil, parsley and garlic powder. Cover with sliced pepperoni, sprinkle with shredded cheese and top with mushrooms. Bake in a 425° oven 15 minutes or until cheese is bubbly.

Variation: Use ½ lb. cooked Italian sausage in place of pepperoni, and add sliced green pepper.

Taco Pita Olé

This is a nice do-it-yourself sandwich for a crowd. Serve with a large salad and fresh fruit.

1 lb. ground beef prepared
   with taco seasoning
2 cups lettuce, shredded
1 cup tomato, chopped
½ cup black olives, chopped

1½ cups cheddar cheese, shredded
¾ cup refried beans
½ cup sour cream
4-6 pita pockets, cut in half

Arrange prepared ground beef, lettuce, tomato, olives, cheddar cheese, refried beans and sour cream in small bowls. Each person fills his own pita pocket with his choice of filling.

South Philadelphia Stromboli Sandwich

Serves 4-6

This hearty calzone-type sandwich is a favorite of the Italians in South Philadelphia. Make it for a football party or for poker night.

1 (1 lb.) loaf frozen bread dough
2 eggs
2 tsp. Dijon mustard
⅓ cup Parmesan cheese
1 tsp. **each** oregano and sweet basil
⅓ lb. thin sliced luncheon meat (ham, salami, pepperoni, turkey or other)
¼ lb. mozzarella cheese, shredded, **or** Monterey Jack
2 tbs. mild onion, finely chopped

Defrost dough and roll it into a 9" x 13" rectangle. Whisk egg, mustard, oregano, sweet basil and cheese together. Spread over dough to within ½" of edges. Layer meats down the center of the long dimension of dough, sprinkle cheese over meats, and then chopped onion. Fold up sides of dough over meats and cheese and crimp edges to seal. Bake in a 425° oven until golden brown, about 20 minutes. Cut in small pieces to serve. Serve warm or at room temperature.

Bread Sticks

This is a fast and delicious recipe for making bread sticks in less than an hour. Bake some in extra long sticks and stand them up in a little pitcher or mug for an edible table centerpiece.

2 pkgs. rapid rise yeast
1 tbs. brown sugar
1½ cups warm water
1 tsp. salt
¼ cup olive oil
3-3½ cups all-purpose flour
1 egg white, beaten with 1 tbs. water
coarse salt or sesame seeds (optional)

In a large bowl, combine yeast, sugar and warm (110°) water. Stir to dissolve yeast and let stand for a few minutes until mixture starts to get bubbly. Add 2 cups of the flour, salt and olive oil. Stir vigorously with a wooden spoon for 3-4 minutes or use a heavy duty mixer with a paddle. Add flour ½ cup at a time and mix until the dough cleans the bowl but is still soft. Turn dough out on a floured board and knead until smooth and satiny. Allow dough to rest for about 5 minutes covered with a towel. Roll into a log about 20" long and cut into 20 equal pieces with a sharp knife. Cover pieces with a towel and allow to rest again for 5 minutes. Roll each piece to the length of your baking sheet, or shorter. Arrange sticks about 1" apart on oiled baking sheets. Allow to rise for about 20 minutes. Brush lightly with egg white mixture. Sprinkle with coarse salt or sesame seeds if desired. Bake in a 300° oven for about 30 minutes until golden brown. Remove to a cooling rack. For very crisp bread sticks, put sticks back into a 250° oven after they have cooled completely and bake for another 20-30 minutes just before serving.

Quick Pizza Crust and Toppings

This recipe makes 1 pizza, 16", or two pizzas, 11" each, and can be ready to bake in an hour.

1 pkg. rapid rise yeast
1 cup warm water
2 tsp. brown sugar

3 cups bread flour **or** all-purpose flour
2 tbs. olive oil
1 tsp. salt

Combine yeast, warm (110°) water and brown sugar in a large mixing bowl. When yeast dissolves and mixture starts to bubble, stir in 2 cups of flour and mix well. Add olive oil and salt and mix until smooth, about 2-3 minutes. Add another ½ cup flour, continuing to mix until dough starts to clean sides of bowl. Turn out on a floured board and knead in remaining flour. Dough will be smooth, satiny and fairly soft. Lightly oil the mixing bowl and return dough to bowl, turning to coat with oil. Cover with a towel or plastic wrap and allow to rise in a warm place until doubled in size, about 30 minutes.

To assemble, roll into one large pizza or 2 smaller ones, and place on a cookie sheet or metal pizza pan. Turn up edges, paint with olive oil and distribute topping ingredients over crust. Bake in a preheated 500° oven for 9-12 minutes until crust is brown and cheese bubbles. Remove from oven and sprinkle with Parmesan cheese. Serve immediately.

Classic Pizza Topping

olive oil
pizza sauce
grated mozzarella, Monterey Jack or fontina cheese
slices of pepperoni, Italian sausage, salami or ham
chopped onion
chopped green pepper
sliced mushrooms
chopped black olives

Roll out crusts and paint with olive oil. Spoon on a thin layer of prepared pizza sauce. Add grated cheese, top with slices of meat, and add vegetables of choice. Bake as directed above.

Carmelized Onion Pizza Topping

2 tbs. butter
1 lb. yellow onions, thinly sliced
1 tsp. dried thyme
⅛ tsp. grated nutmeg

1 cup white wine
1 cup Gruyere cheese, shredded
2 tbs. Parmesan cheese

Melt butter in a heavy skillet. Add onions, thyme and nutmeg. Cover and cook over very low heat for about 45 minutes, stirring occasionally. Onions should be very soft, but not brown. Add wine and allow to simmer uncovered until all the liquid has evaporated, about 45 minutes. Cool before using.

To assemble pizza, roll out pizza crusts, turn up edges and paint with olive oil. Distribute Gruyere cheese over crust to within ½" of edge. Distribute onion mixture evenly over cheese. Bake in a 500° oven for 9-12 minutes until crust is brown and cheese bubbles. Remove from oven and sprinkle with Parmesan cheese. Serve immediately. Onions can be made ahead and kept in the refrigerator for a few days, or frozen. Defrost before using.

Other Quick Pizza Toppings

- Brush rolled out dough with full-flavored olive oil, top with thinly sliced red onion rings, finely minced garlic, chopped fresh sweet basil leaves and 3-4 tbs. freshly grated Parmesan cheese.
- Brush rolled out dough with full-flavored olive oil, top with ½ cup grated mozzarella cheese, ¼ tsp. hot red pepper flakes, 2-3 green onions, thinly sliced, and 2 tbs. Parmesan cheese. Top hot pizza with fresh ripe tomato pieces (1 medium tomato, peeled, seeded and chopped).
- Brush rolled out dough with full-flavored olive oil, top with ½ cup grated mozzarella cheese, thinly sliced red onion rings, 1 tsp. chopped fresh oregano and a few hot red pepper flakes.
- Brush rolled out dough with full-flavored olive oil and top with ½ cup grated mozzarella cheese. Cut ½ green bell pepper, ½ red bell pepper and ½ medium onion into strips. Cook in a microwave for 2 minutes; drain well. Cook 6 mushrooms, thinly sliced, in microwave for 2 minutes; drain well. Distribute vegetables over pizza.

Sweets

Men love sweets. For many of them, a meal isn't a meal without some kind of dessert. In our surveys, men listed many kinds of desserts, but the most frequently listed favorite dessert was pie, especially apple, cherry and lemon. And next in popularity was cake, with chocolate heading the list. Third place was ice cream with cookies, chocolate chip, brownies and oatmeal, in that order. We've included these three categories (we've left out ice cream and settled on the cookies) in our Sweets section. And finally, although it didn't fit into one of our categories, we've added **Dan's Rich and Easy Chocolate Mousse** just because.

Grandma Lee's Buttermilk Cake

2 loaves

This cake is a favorite for generations of men in the Lee family.

1 cup margarine
3 cups sugar
5-6 eggs (1 cup)
3 cups flour

½ tsp. soda
½ tsp. salt
1 cup buttermilk

In a medium bowl, cream margarine and sugar until light and fluffy. Add eggs and continue beating 10 minutes. In a small bowl, stir flour, soda and salt together. Add to creamed mixture ⅓ at a time, alternately with buttermilk. Bake in 2 lightly greased 9" x 5" loaf pans at 350° for 1 hour. Allow to cool in pans for 10 minutes. Invert on a rack to cool.

Strawberry Shortcake

Serves 4

Strawberry shortcake rates high with men and this old-fashioned shortcake recipe is equally good with strawberries, peaches or raspberries.

2 cups biscuit mix
½ cup milk
2 tbs. sugar
2 tbs. butter, melted

1 tsp. sugar
2 baskets strawberries, washed, stemmed
sweetened whipped cream

Combine biscuit mix with milk, sugar and butter. Dough should be soft enough to drop from a spoon. Divide in quarters and drop from a spoon on an ungreased baking sheet. Sprinkle tops of shortcakes with 1 tsp. sugar and bake at 425° for 10-12 minutes, or until shortcakes are lightly browned and firm to the touch. Let cool before cutting in half and filling with prepared strawberries. Cut the prettiest half of the strawberries in slices. Mash the rest with 2-3 tbs. sugar. Add sliced strawberries and allow to marinate for 15 minutes, or up to 2 hours in the refrigerator. Put a spoonful of strawberries on the bottom half of each shortcake, replace the top and spoon strawberries over. Top with sweetened whipped cream.

Irish Whiskey Cake

Mrs. Murphy has made this for her husband for 54 years. Your favorite fella might stick around that long if you give it a try. On the other hand, he might go visit Mrs. Murphy.

1 (18.2 ozs.) pkg. yellow cake mix
1 (3.75 ozs.) instant vanilla pudding
3 eggs
½ cup whiskey
½ cup cold water
½ cup vegetable oil
½ cup nuts, chopped

In a large mixing bowl, blend cake mix, pudding mix, eggs, whiskey, water and oil. Stir in nuts. Pour into a well greased and floured bundt pan. Bake at 350° for 50-60 minutes. Allow to cool 10 minutes in pan and then invert onto a rack to cool.

Pineapple Upside Down Cake

This cake has won popularity contests for years. It goes together quickly using a cake mix.

1 (9 ozs.) pkg. yellow cake mix
3 tbs. butter, melted
⅓ cup brown sugar

1 (8 ozs.) can pineapple slices, drained
¼ cup pecan halves

Mix cake as directed on package. Place melted butter in an 8" x 8" square baking pan. Distribute brown sugar evenly over butter. Arrange drained pineapple slices over brown sugar and distribute pecan halves, rounded side down. Pour prepared cake mix over pineapple and nuts. Bake at 350° for about 40-45 minutes, or until a cake tester or toothpick comes out clean. Remove to a cooling rack and allow to cool for about 5 minutes, and then invert onto a serving plate.

Alex ▶
Sweet Cherry Pie (page 162)

Pumpkin Cake

Serves 15

This is a great cake for a potluck or a soup and dessert supper.

1 (29 ozs.) can pumpkin
1 cup sugar
1 (12 ozs.) can evaporated milk
1 tsp. cinnamon
⅛ tsp. cloves
¼ tsp. nutmeg
3 eggs
1 (18.2 ozs.) pkg. yellow cake mix
1 cup walnuts, chopped
¾ cup butter or margarine, melted

Frosting:
1 (3 ozs.) pkg. cream cheese, softened
1 cup powdered sugar
1 (8 ozs.) tub whipped topping
½ tsp. vanilla

In a medium bowl, combine pumpkin, sugar, evaporated milk, spices and eggs. Pour into a 9″ x 13″ lightly greased baking pan. Sprinkle dry cake mix over mixture. Top with chopped walnuts, patting topping down. Pour melted butter or margarine over all. Bake at 350° for 1 hour. Allow to cool in pan for 10 minutes; invert cake onto a platter. Cool before frosting. In a small bowl, mix frosting ingredients and spread evenly on cake.

◄ **Jeff**
Double Chocolate Brownies (page 168)

Ultra Chocolate Cake

Serves 15

Chocolate lovers dream about this kind of cake, rich and moist, with a big chocolate taste.

3 ozs. unsweetened chocolate
½ cup butter
2½ cups brown sugar
3 eggs
2¼ cups cake flour, sifted

2 tsp. salt
½ cup buttermilk
1 cup boiling water
2 tsp. vanilla

Melt chocolate and set aside to cool slightly. Butter and lightly flour a 9" x 13" baking pan. In a mixing bowl, cream butter and brown sugar; add eggs one at a time, beating after each addition. Stir in melted chocolate. Sift together sifted cake flour, baking soda and salt. Add a little of the flour to chocolate mixture alternately with buttermilk, ending with flour. Mix in boiling water and vanilla. Pour into prepared cake pan and bake at 375° for 35-40 minutes, or until cake tester comes out clean. Remove to a cooling rack and cool completely before icing with the recipe below.

Chocolate Cream Cheese Icing

3 ozs. cream cheese
3 ozs. unsweetened baking chocolate
1 tsp. vanilla
2 tsp. dark rum
1 (1 lb.) box powdered sugar, sifted
3 tbs. heavy cream

In a medium bowl, melt chocolate over boiling water. When just soft, add cream cheese and beat well. Stir in vanilla and rum. Add powdered sugar, beating until smooth. If frosting seems to be thick, thin with a little cream so it is easy to spread.

Malcolm's Apple Cake

Serves 15

Malcolm says serve it warm with ice cream or whipped cream or whipped topping.

4 cups tart cooking apples, diced
2 cups sugar
½ cup vegetable oil
2 eggs
2 tsp. vanilla

2 tsp. cinnamon
½ tsp. salt
2 tsp. baking soda
2 cups all-purpose flour
1 cup walnuts, chopped

In a medium bowl, mix apples and sugar until well coated. In another bowl, mix oil, eggs and vanilla. Add to apples. Mix dry ingredients and add to apple mixture. Pour into a greased 9" x 13" baking pan. Bake at 350° for 1 hour. Serve warm.

French Silk Pie

Serves 6-8

Ed sent us this recipe for a pie so rich, so smooth it melts in your mouth.

1 cup butter
1 cup sugar
3 ozs. unsweetened chocolate, melted, cooled
1 tsp. vanilla
4 eggs
1 baked pie shell, 9"
whipped topping
semisweet chocolate bar

Cream butter and sugar. Add melted chocolate and vanilla. Add 2 eggs and beat at high speed for 5 minutes. Add 2 more eggs and beat an additional 5 minutes. Be sure to beat for the entire 10 minutes. Pour into baked pie shell and chill at least 1 hour. Garnish with dollops of whipped topping. Shave chocolate over all.

Sweet Cherry Pie

When fresh cherries are in the market, make this wonderful pie for your best man.

Filling:
¾ cup sugar
2 tbs. quick-cooking tapioca
½ tsp. cinnamon
5 cups sweet cherries, pitted
2 tbs. lemon juice

In a small bowl, stir together sugar, tapioca and cinnamon. Combine cherries and lemon juice in a large bowl; sprinkle with sugar mixture. Stir cherries until lightly coated with sugar. Set aside while preparing pastry.

Flaky Pastry:
2½ cups all-purpose flour
½ tsp. salt
½ cup cold butter
⅓ cup vegetable shortening
4-6 tbs. cold water
1 tbs. butter
1-2 tbs. heavy cream

In a large bowl, mix flour and salt. Cut in butter and shortening until mixture is crumbly and resembles coarse meal. Sprinkle in water 1 tbs. at a time and mix lightly with a fork until dough begins to cling together. With your hands, press dough into two flattened disks of equal size.

Roll out ½ pastry between two pieces of waxed paper to fit a 9" pie pan. Ease pastry into pan and trim edge even with rim. Fill with cherry mixture. Dot with 1 tbs. butter. Roll out remaining pastry to fit top of pie pan; cover and trim to rim. Press top crust to bottom crust with tines of a fork. Brush top crust with cream and cut a design to let out steam. Bake at 450° for 10 minutes. Reduce heat to 350° and bake for 30-35 minutes or until filling bubbles up. Serve warm or at room temperature, with whipped cream or ice cream if desired.

Mom's Sour Cream Apple Pie

This recipe is quick and a great favorite of all the men we know.

Pie Crust:
1¼ cups all-purpose flour
½ cup cold unsalted butter
2 tbs. sour cream
¼ tsp. salt

Combine flour and butter in a food processor bowl or cut in butter with a pastry blender. Add sour cream and salt and process until mixture forms a ball, adding a little more sour cream if necessary. Roll out between pieces of waxed paper and place in a 9" pie plate. Bake at 375° for 20 minutes until firm and very lightly browned. Remove from oven and let cool while making filling.

Filling:
3 large egg yolks
½ cup sour cream
¾ cup sugar
¼ cup flour
¼ tsp. salt
½ tsp. cinnamon
¼ tsp. nutmeg
grated lemon rind from 1 lemon
3 large cooking apples, peeled, cored, thinly sliced

Combine egg yolks, sour cream, sugar, flour, salt, cinnamon, nutmeg and lemon rind in a large bowl. Beat until mixture is well blended and lemon colored. Pour about ⅓ of the mixture in bottom of baked pie crust. Top with sliced apples and remaining egg mixture. Bake at 375° for 45-50 minutes until top has puffed and lightly browned.

Freezer Lemon Pie

Another big winner with men, this silky lemon pie can be made ahead and kept in the freezer.

Cookie Crumb Crust:
½ cup melted butter
3 tbs. brown sugar
1 tsp. grated lemon rind
2 cups vanilla wafers, crushed

Combine melted butter, sugar and lemon rind. Stir in cookie crumbs. Press into a buttered 9" pie pan. Chill in refrigerator for 15 minutes to set. Bake at 325° for 10 minutes until crust is crisp. Allow to cool before filling.

Lemon Filling:
1 egg
¾ cup sugar
1 tbs. flour
1 tbs. grated lemon rind
⅓ cup lemon juice
1 cup heavy cream

Combine egg, sugar and flour in the top of a double boiler. Stir in lemon rind and lemon juice, mixing well. Cook over boiling water until mixture thickens. Remove and place top of double boiler in a bowl of cold water. Allow to cool to room temperature. Whip cream until stiff. Fold into cooled lemon mixture and pour into baked cookie crust. Freeze until firm, 4-6 hours or longer. Remove from freezer and place in refrigerator about 30 minutes before serving.

Fabulous Frozen Peanut Butter Pie

Serves 8

Peanut butter is another winner with men. Here is peanut butter turned into a rich pie, garnished with chocolate. Allow to stand at room temperature 20 minutes before cutting.

½ cup sugar
1 (8 ozs.) pkg. cream cheese, room temperature
¾ cup chunky peanut butter
1 tsp. vanilla
¼ cup milk
1 cup heavy cream, whipped **or** 1 (8 ozs.) tub whipped topping
1 graham cracker crust, 9" **or** chocolate crumb or pastry shell
½ cup whipping cream, whipped
2-3 tbs. chocolate sauce
¼ cup peanuts, chopped

In a small mixing bowl, beat sugar, cream cheese, peanut butter and vanilla until smooth. Add milk gradually, mixing well. Fold whipped cream or whipped topping into mixture. Pour into pie shell. Freeze at least 4 hours. Wrap well once frozen, if planning longer freezer storage. To serve, garnish with whipped cream mounds, drizzle with chocolate sauce and sprinkle with peanuts.

Variation: Use this same filling without the crust to make peanut butter parfaits. Simply layer filling, alternating layers with whipped cream, chocolate and nuts.

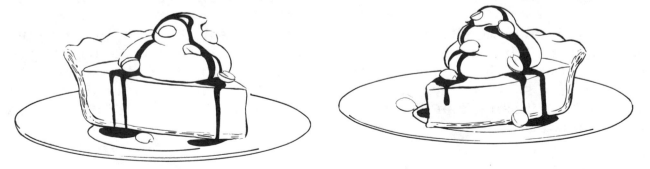

Texas Pecan Pie

Serves 6

We found pecan pie on our surveys many times. Rick isn't from Texas, but he says the pecans are. Since he's an ex-defensive lineman, we choose to believe him.

3 eggs
⅔ cup sugar
dash salt
1 cup dark corn syrup

⅓ cup melted butter
1 cup pecan halves
1 unbaked 9" pie shell

In a medium bowl, beat eggs thoroughly with sugar, salt, corn syrup and melted butter. Add pecans and pour into pastry shell. Bake in a 350° oven for 50 minutes or until knife inserted in center comes out clean. Cool before cutting. Serve with whipped topping.

Saucepan Chocolate Chip Bar Cookies

30 cookies

Marybeth makes these for her husband Lon, but not too often, because he can eat them all in an hour.

2⅔ cups sifted all-purpose flour
2½ tsp. baking powder
½ tsp. salt
⅔ cup butter **or** margarine

2¼ cups brown sugar
3 eggs
1 cup nuts, chopped
12 ozs. semisweet chocolate pieces

In a medium bowl, sift flour, baking powder and salt together. In a medium saucepan, melt butter. Stir in brown sugar, allow to cool slightly and add eggs, one at a time, beating well after each addition. Add sifted ingredients and nuts. Allow to cool slightly. Stir in chocolate chips. Pour into a generously greased 10½" x 15½" baking pan. Bake at 350° for 25-30 minutes. Cut into squares when almost cool.

No Bake Breakfast Boosters

24 cookies

Start your man off to a great healthy start with these "good for him" cookies.

½ cup honey
½ cup chunky peanut butter
½ cup instant nonfat dry milk powder
2½ cups Oat Bran Flakes cereal, coarsely crushed **or** other cereal flakes
½ cup seedless raisins

In a small saucepan, heat honey and peanut butter. Stir to blend. Remove from heat and stir in dry milk powder. Fold in crushed cereal and raisins. Drop by large tablespoonfuls onto waxed paper. Cool to room temperature and then store in refrigerator.

Variation: Add ½ cup of dried fruits, dates or walnuts.

Oatmeal Cookies

5 dozen cookies

Oatmeal cookies ranked third in our survey.

¾ cup vegetable shortening
1 cup brown sugar, packed
½ cup granulated sugar
1 egg
¼ cup water
1 tsp. vanilla extract

3 cups rolled oats
¾ cup all-purpose flour
¼ cup wheat germ
1 tsp. salt
1 tsp. baking soda
1 cup raisins **or** dried fruit bits

In a large bowl, beat shortening, sugars, egg, water and vanilla until creamy and smooth. In a medium bowl, combine oats, flour, wheat germ, salt and soda. Add to creamed mixture and mix well. Stir in raisins. Drop by rounded teaspoonfuls onto a lightly greased cookie sheet. Bake at 350° for 12-15 minutes.

Lemon Cookies

You can have a sweet treat ready for him in minutes.

1 (18.2) pkg. lemon cake mix
8 ozs. frozen whipped topping, thawed
1 egg
powdered sugar

In a medium bowl, mix cake mix, whipped topping and egg until combined. Roll into 1½" balls and place on a cookie sheet sprayed with nonstick vegetable spray. Bake at 350° for 8-10 minutes. While cookies are still warm, roll in powdered sugar.

Double Chocolate Brownies

Sinfully delicious, incredibly chocolaty, unbelievably rich. Developed by Ellie and Dennis, owners of "Hot Pots" kitchen store. They have male customers who drive a long way for this little bit of sin.

1½ cups unbleached flour
½ tsp. baking soda
¼ tsp. salt
1 tsp. vanilla
¾ cup brown sugar
¾ cup white sugar
⅔ cup shortening
3½ cups chocolate chips
4 eggs
½ cup walnuts, chopped
¼ cup hot water

In a large mixing bowl, mix flour, baking soda, salt and vanilla together. In a medium bowl, combine brown sugar and white sugar. Melt shortening (microwave 2 minutes on low) and stir in 2 cups chocolate chips, reserving 1½ cups for later. Stir in hot water. Add this mixture to sugars and stir well. Slightly beat 4 eggs and add to sugar/chocolate mixture. Add chocolate mixture to flour mixture and blend well. Stir in remaining 1½ cups chocolate chips and nuts. Spread into an 11" x 15" greased cake pan. Bake at 350° for 35-40 minutes.

Chocolate Peanut Butter Chip Cookies

48 cookies

Stick a Chocolate Peanut Butter Chip Cookie in his mouth and he'll follow you anywhere.

8 ozs. semisweet chocolate
3 tbs. butter **or** margarine
1 (14 ozs.) can sweetened condensed milk
2 cups biscuit mix
1 tsp. vanilla extract
1 cup peanut butter flavored chips

In a large saucepan over low heat, melt chocolate and margarine in sweetened condensed milk (or melt in microwave). Add biscuit mix and vanilla and beat with a mixer until well blended. Cool. Stir in peanut butter chips. Shape into 1½" balls. Place about 2" apart on an ungreased baking sheet. Bake at 350° for 6-8 minutes.

Chewy Brown Sugar Brownies

Serves 9

Even though chocolate is a favorite among men, Bill likes to bake and enjoy these nonchocolate gems.

1 cup light brown sugar
⅓ cup shortening
1 egg
¼ tsp. salt
1 tsp. baking powder
¾ cup all-purpose flour
¼ cup whole wheat flour
½ cup nuts, chopped
⅓ cup apple, shredded **or** carrot or zucchini

Coat a 9" square pan with cooking spray. Cream brown sugar and shortening. Add egg and beat until fluffy. Stir salt, baking powder and flours together. Add to brown sugar, shortening and egg mixture. Stir in chopped nuts and apple. Pour into prepared pan and bake in a 350° oven for 25 minutes or until brownies are lightly browned and begin to pull away from sides of pan. Cool. Cut into 25 small squares or 9 dessert squares. Perfect with ice cream.

Dan's Rich and Easy Chocolate Mousse

Serves 4-6

This is favored because it takes just one bowl and the ingredients don't have to be measured exactly.

12 ozs. cream cheese
1 cup sugar
1-2 tsp. vanilla
½ cup cocoa
1½ cups heavy cream, whipped

Beat cream cheese, sugar, vanilla and cocoa until smooth. Fold in all but 2 tbs. whipped cream until well blended. Pour into 4-6 dessert dishes. Garnish with remaining whipped cream and shaved chocolate.

Index

Mary Anne Bauer has been a long-time Pacific Northwest television favorite on *AM Northwest,* and has appeared on such national shows as Gary Collins' *Hour Magazine.* You may have seen her on Seattle's *Good Company, AM San Francisco,* New York City's *Morning Show, AM Buffalo,* or cable television. She's the author of **What's for Breakfast?,** nine other cookbooks and a food columnist for several newspapers.